It's Okay

A MEMOIR

Brendan Heaney

innovativeink
PUBLISHING
A Division of Kendall Hunt

www.innovativeinkpublishing.com
Send all inquiries to:
4050 Westmark Drive
Dubuque, IA 52004-1840

Print ISBN: 979-8-3851-2824-2
Ebook ISBN: 979-8-3851-2825-9

Published in the United States of America

To Molly

"Just Do It"

I sat in my seat getting quite bored,
Everyone else was getting an award.
Cathy got an award for her good looks,
Brian earned a prize for reading lots of books.
I sat and I sat watching names being read.
Holy Cow!
They even awarded that nitwit named Fred.

Then there was Sally
Who got a trophy for dancing in the ballet.
Then came Rick -
I guess you get recognized for never getting sick.
Then came Joe,
He was awarded for plants he did grow.
Oh, don't forget about Flo,
Apparently, she was really good in some show.
They awarded that gymnast named Wendy,
My God, that girl sure can get bendy.
They gave a medal to the new kid Jose.
What Crap! I sat there thinking "No Way!"
Then came Helen!
Don't they know she's a felon?
Then there was Paul…
…really? For throwing a ball?
Oh, yeah, then there was Pat,
Well, I guess he *is* pretty good at swinging his bat.

Each person got a speech that made them sound great.
One kid even got an award for never being late.
Jenny got a trophy for her positive attitude,
I sat there realizing I was in a terrible mood.
Bob was awarded for being patriotic and
Here I was becoming incredibly neurotic.
All these people who got up on stage,
I could feel boiling inside of me a volcanic little rage.

Were they better than me?
Just how could that be?

Each person would smile and receive a handshake.
This entire event seemed so phony and fake.
I got more upset when they awarded a teacher.
Don't they know she's a hideous creature?
They awarded a janitor for being so neat and so clean.
Can't they see he's also really mean?
They gave some girl an award for playing her flute,
I told myself I didn't give one single hoot.

But person after person came up to that stage,
All except for me, sitting like an angry little sage.

Oh, how did these people become so highly rated?
Maybe I would know…if only I ever participated.

Acknowledgments

I would like to thank my students. Throughout the years many of you have directly inspired me to write this book. I'd also like to thank my friend Beth for being the initial editor for me and offering stylistic advice. Editing is often thankless. This book is better because of your amazing help.

I'd like to thank all my friends throughout my life. I don't have many, but the ones I have are awesome. One of the secrets to happiness is to surround yourself with good, positive people. My friends have taken care of that. Thank you. You are all blessings that I cherish.

It is essential that I acknowledge the family I grew up with. This book is your story as much as it is mine. I'm sure we all remember these events a little differently from one another. That's how memory works. Please know that every word was written with love and affection. This is *our* story. I wouldn't change any of the past, no matter how screwed up it might have been at the time. I apologize for any embellishments, inaccuracies, or unintended falsehoods. As I say throughout the book, I have told these stories the way I remember them. I'm not sure how they really happened or even if they happened at all. Too much time has passed, but thoughts and feelings remain. That's what I tried to capture.

Finally, I want to thank the family I've built; my wife, Molly, and my two daughters, Jenna and Mara. You are everything to me. You all inspire me more than anything. This book is about things that happened to me, but it's also filled with messages for you. Read this knowing that my words are always there for you.

Molly, I hope you read this and understand why you are the perfect woman for me. You've always "gotten" me and my quirks. Hopefully, this explains some of the things you already know just a little more. To Jenna and Mara, this is a story about growing up. With a sense of wonder and awe I've watched you guys grow up. Your childhood was quite different from mine. That's a good thing. I want you to have your own stories that you can be proud of and write down some day. Remember that life is not always fair, it isn't always easy and a lot of the time it hurts. That's okay. It's an adventure. It's best when you can find a way to laugh through it all.

Introduction

At twenty-two years old I found myself paralyzed with a sense of panic. My career as a teacher had just begun and something was immediately apparent; I sucked. No. I didn't suck. I really sucked.

I had grown up in a family of teachers. My father taught English, my mother taught every discipline of science imaginable, and my older brother taught history. One of the quirky things in my life is that my education entailed having *all* of them as my teachers. That's right. They weren't just mom, dad, and brother. They were also my classroom instructors all through high school. It was like a weird version of being home-schooled. Having been born into a family of educators, there was a notion that teaching was in the blood. The only one to escape this fate was my twin brother who became a police officer. I, on the other hand, would reluctantly fall in line with the rest of my kin. I didn't resist it by kicking and screaming or anything, but the idea of teaching just didn't seem appealing. I feared I'd be an embarrassment to the rest of my clan.

The bar had been set high as my family members were all successful. They were good teachers and I didn't seem to be blessed with their talent. I knew what good teaching looked like but was concerned that a necessary set of skills had eluded me. Oh, the shame! Again, I *never* had any intention of becoming a teacher. Mostly, I just wanted to spend all my time reading books. My lack of self-confidence made the prospect of being a full-time student much more alluring. The "real world" scared me and spending the rest of my life in a dusty old library was more appealing than anything.

Unfortunately, reality is a harsh master, and one must face it eventually. It was unavoidable. The career of a teacher would prove to track me down despite all my efforts trying to escape it. Having massive insecurity about interacting with people, I initially had other career plans. I briefly set my sights on delivering mail for a living or roofing houses. Anything sounded better than facing hordes of students, parents, and administrators. I had zero confidence in my ability to face a classroom full of kids, but I also knew I'd have to grow up and bite the proverbial bullet. It was a crisis and I had to find *something* that could be called a career. After all, I was a college graduate and no longer a kid.

My relatives had one piece of advice: Go into the family trade.

"You won't get rich, but people will respect you."

That's what my father told me. How true and untrue, unfortunately, those words would prove to be. It was finally time to stop worrying and come up with a plan for my future and a decision was made. With no better options, I found myself attending graduate school to become an English teacher. Things moved pretty fast from there. Before I knew it, I was employed by people myopic enough not to notice my lack of talent.

All things considered, it was a miracle they gave me a job. As mentioned, I was terrible. Thankfully, improvement would occur with time. At first, I had no business being at the head of a classroom. Anxiety and dread were my constant companions and every day of work required putting on a fake persona; a "teacher mask." Fake it until you make it was my motto. Act like a teacher until you are one. Operating on a "one day at a time" basis, I survived my first year. That's what life felt like, *survival.* My second year of teaching wasn't much better. But, if God granted me with anything, it's a strong will to persevere through painful situations. Resilience became the mantra, and I made it through the second year.

With two years of teaching under my belt, there wasn't a heck of a lot of improvement. The content was fine, but it was a struggle connecting with students. They simply didn't seem to give a crap about anything I was teaching. This wasn't sustainable and my mind was full of questions. What to do? Maybe the family business wasn't for me. Could I get better? If so, how?

Advice poured in from colleagues and family members. "Stick with it" was the common refrain.

"Things will get better."

"Keep plugging away."

"Stop being such a wimp."

It seemed that talent might have eluded me and desperation set in. Counting my losses and quitting felt like a good option. Then, in my third year, something big happened. An epiphany. One day, instead of teaching a pre-planned lesson, I decided to tell a funny story. It was a story from my childhood and the students responded. Heck, they didn't just respond, they were laughing. They were on the ground in hysterics. A magic trick had taken place and a spark ignited. There had been an ace hiding in my back pocket. When I needed it most, I found something valuable: Stories! *My* stories! And, boy, did I have stories.

I can't remember what the first personal story I told to a class full of bored teenagers was about. However, I do remember noticing a few things in telling it. First, the students were in the palm of my hand. They were eager to hear about my experiences. Second, they laughed. How awesome! Maybe the actual story was amusing. Maybe it was the way it was told that was funny. Maybe it was both. But what a rush it was to get a laugh from the harshest audience in the world…indifferent teenagers. It felt great. Was this teaching? It didn't matter. Something worked. Eureka!

What happened next was amazing. Students began asking for more. How could I say no to a room full of eager faces begging for a story? I suddenly became a craftsman, a raconteur, a peddler of tales. Soon my classroom became like an open-mic night at a comedy club. My profession began to make sense and I got good at it. It wasn't necessary to put on a "teacher mask" anymore. Best of all, telling my stories to legions of students allowed me to realize something essential, my identity.

Over the years the students who heard my tales kept telling me to write a book. Even the kids who hated reading would say they would love to read *my* book. In a way, this memoir is for them. But there's more to it than that. This is a book for everybody. It's not about me (please forgive anything that seems like an ego trip) so much as it's about childhood. Growing up is about one thing overall, survival. It's a small miracle that any of us get out of it alive. My childhood was no better or worse than anyone else's. It was just full of adventures. Some of them were fun. Some were funny. Some were scary. Some were dangerous. Many were painful. I survived these experiences and lived to tell the tale. Maybe that's something just about anybody can relate to.

But, more than being an adventure, growing up is mysterious. At best, it's a magic trick. Gradually, but way too quickly, our child-selves disappear into a cloud of smoke and we emerge as adults. Poof! What the hell just happened? We can only look back in a state of perpetual wonder and hope we aren't turned to salt. Mostly, our childhood experiences don't make sense while they're happening. It's only after the smoke clears that we find a reason for everything that occurred. These pages pay tribute to this idea. Finding reason and purpose is a perpetual journey. After all, the adventure doesn't stop when we reach adulthood.

If we're lucky we never *really* grow up.

Note to the Reader

I can't be sure how much of what I remember from my childhood is true. I'm only sure that I remember things a particular way and my memory *feels* true. Memory is funny like that. The older you get the less you know, but the stronger you believe. You must rely on *unreliable* memory. It's an act of faith, I guess. The stories of my youth are full of surreal and quirky details and I've come to terms with them. Exactly what happened really doesn't matter as much as how it made me feel, and how it continues to make me feel. I remember the *feelings* more than I remember anything else. The memory of those emotions is what exists in my stories. Truth lives in the emotions.

The events in these pages are *based* on true stories. I'll be the first to admit that they may not have happened exactly as I've told them. This is just *my* memory of things. When it comes to the past, I would never presume to be sure of anything. Hell, maybe none of it really happened and it was all just a dream. Who knows? What I do know is that I have been inspired by family and friends to tell these tales to the best of my ability. I have changed most of the names "to protect the innocent" as they say. I have nothing but love and gratitude to everyone involved.

This book was written because one of my students gave me homework. The assignment has been finished…I hope I pass.

1

An Origin Story

"Whatever you do, don't see *Jaws!*" That's what my mother was told the summer I was born. It's horrible advice if you ask me. It's one of the greatest movies ever made. I watch it repeatedly and never get tired of it. In fact, whenever I turn on the TV and catch the film halfway through, I'm compelled to keep watching it until the conclusion. It doesn't matter that I've seen it a ridiculous number of times. For some reason I can never get sick of a cinematic masterpiece starring an unstoppable killer shark.

In 1975, *Jaws* was the first "blockbuster." Audiences were literally lining up around street corners to see a movie about people in a Cape Cod town being attacked by a giant fish. Apparently, this wasn't just your ordinary movie. There was a growing buzz as crowds of movie-goers discovered it wasn't for the faint of heart. The movie was so intense that it came with a warning. If you were a nervous person or in a delicate condition, you should avoid it at all costs. My pregnant mother's obstetrician gave her this same advice. He told her that seeing the film might cause her to have a miscarriage. The doctor held a Victorian attitude concerning the fragility of women and imagined young ladies all over the country swooning in the aisles at the sight of a shark ripping people to pieces. Nonetheless, my mother was a good patient and took her doctor's advice. She never got a chance to see *Jaws*.

My mom may have missed the best movie of the year, but one thing she didn't miss was a trip to the X-ray room after a bizarre incident in the middle of the night. Her pregnancy had been uneventful for the first few months but that was just the calm before the storm. At a certain point, she had become uncomfortably pregnant. One evening she was lying on her back, trying to fall asleep, when she suddenly noticed her very large belly expanding on both sides. STRETCH! It was horrific. Imagine a balloon full of restless puppies trying to escape all at once. She thought she was going to be pushed wide open from within. After what must have seemed like a terrifying eternity wondering what the hell was happening to her body, the expansion stopped and then receded. It freaked her out. What kind of *Rosemary's Baby* monster was growing inside her? She had been pregnant with my older brother six years prior and during that pregnancy had never experienced anything like this. This was not normal. What was wrong with this baby? She was nervous enough to head to the doctor the next day.

There was a mystery that needed solving. What kind of creature was living inside my mother's uterus? Furthermore, how would she find out? The answer: *X-rays!* The infinite medical wisdom of the day was to blast expecting mothers with X-rays to investigate any concerns. I have no idea if damage was done and I certainly wasn't born with any superpowers. It's possible that it may have created a little neurosis of some kind. Either way, what was done was done. The good news was that the X-rays provided a solution to the mystery of the amazing expanding baby. It turns out there were two of me. Twins. Holy Crap!

I can only imagine the look on my neurotic and unprepared father's face when he found out he was getting two for the price of one. I'm positive he got unbelievably drunk after hearing the amazing news of siring twins. Most likely his drinking accelerated over the next few days from the shock of it all, but he knew he would eventually have to sober up. Within months, two fraternal boys would be squeezed into the world and he would have to be responsible.

It's lucky neither of my parents could see into the future.

Our birth would be remembered by my parents as a nightmarishly hellish event. It was always told and retold as if it was a myth; my family never had a problem with hyperbolic expression. Furthermore, the story of our birth was told to us with what felt like an agenda, like we were being reminded that we should feel lucky to be alive. Sometimes, when listening to the tale, it also felt like we were being accused of having done something wrong, as if it was our fault the event was so traumatic. I would come to know of my birthing in the similar way that Christians think of the agony of the crucifixion. We were meant to take meaning from the suffering of others. There was no cruelty from Roman soldiers, nor was there a gory crucifixion, but there certainly was pain. According to the legend, my mother's agonizing labor went on for days. At one point, during the ordeal, she needed a rest and collapsed on the cold hospital floor with the side of her face against the tiles. She slept that way for hours. When she woke, something was different. One side of her face was frozen and unable to move. She had developed permanent Bell's palsy. But that was just the start. There was also drama in the waiting room.

In 1975 husbands didn't often go into the birthing room with their significant others. My father can be imagined pacing the floor of the waiting room, probably a little gassed up from his drink of choice, smoking cigarettes and praying to God. He was overwhelmingly freaked out from the notion of bringing home not one, but two babies. He was alone with his neurosis waiting for any news coming from the delivery room while my mother was experiencing the worst pain of her life. Poor guy.

It had taken my parents six years to decide to have another baby. My older brother was described as a toddler Adolf Hitler and his temperament had given them pause. They were understandably skittish about the prospect of re-doing the whole baby thing. What if the next baby turned out to be a Mussolini or a Stalin? Considering this, it's likely my twin and I were a complete accident. Regardless, my parents were stressed about the future. How would the double trouble of two babies impact the fragile family dynamic?

Picture a young father, a man with a history of serious neurosis, pacing back and forth in the hospital's waiting room. Here comes Dr. X-ray with a serious look on his face.

"I'm afraid I have bad news. We've lost one of the babies…I'm sorry. We're trying to save the other one."

Ughhhh. My father goes into shock and panic. He is alone and ill-equipped to deal with this news. He sits down in the waiting room with his head in his hands and begins praying like he's never prayed before. Within the next hour, the doctor comes back with an even more serious look on his face.

"I'm afraid I have more bad news. We've lost the other baby…I'm so sorry. Now we're trying to focus on saving your wife. The strain may have proved too much for her."

I have no idea how my father coped with this. The booze he assuredly drank prior to going to the hospital must have anesthetized him from a total collapse, but somehow, he didn't have a complete meltdown. He sat defeated but continued to pray. Each minute that ticked by was agonizing. A devout Catholic, my father clutched his rosary beads saying prayer after prayer. How would he be able to manage as a single father? After an hour of anguish, the doctor came back with a strange look on his face.

"Would you like to see your sons? We can have them wheeled out for you."

My father didn't know what to say. The last thing he was told had given him the firm expectation that he had lost his wife and his two unborn sons. Was it protocol to wheel out two dead babies? Before he knew it, two carts were headed his way with two unexpectedly alive and squirming newborns. What the hell? These babies were alive and kicking. Surprise!!

Some might think the doctor was either inept or bad at communication. I'd just like to believe that he had his hands full, and the intensity of the moment caused some confusion with the messaging. It's hard to imagine what must have happened in the delivery room, but somehow everyone pulled through. It had been chaotic and terrifying, and the doctor's haste had caused a cruel lapse in effective communication with my terribly neurotic father. C'est la vie.

In the moment of seeing two crying little angry raisins looking up at him, my old man had a mixture of emotions; a combination of relief, joy, terror, wonder, and responsibility. I can only imagine the immortal words of Chief Brodie in *Jaws* running though his mind.

"We're gonna need a bigger boat."

I never met Dr. X-ray. He remains a mythical figure in my mind. Everyone has people in their lives they won't remember, but without them your own life wouldn't be possible. Everything about the act of being born is amazing and we all have stories about the day of our birth…our very own origin stories. I have a teacher friend who begins every school year explaining to students the true miracle of their existence by breaking down the odds of one out of billions of sperm winning the race to fertilize an egg. You won the race! You hit the lottery! Now you get to live your adventure. Now you get to be you. But just *who* are you? My twin brother and I had tied. We both broke the tape at the same time. The birthing process was difficult and farcical, but it would prove to fit in with everything else that would come after. Themes of humor, pain and miscommunication were established along with a sense that, no matter what, things would turn out okay.

The struggle of a long and painful labor had wrecked the unfortunate body of my mother. I'm not sure how many agonized hours she was in the delivery room doing all the things expecting mothers have to do. I know my twin counterpart was not positioned well and the doctor had to do a lot of abnormal internal manual maneuvering required with a breech baby. She never talked about the details too much, but I know it was excruciating. It was very touch and go but she fought the good fight and pushed two infants into the world. I came first and four minutes later my fraternal brother, Jered, came out. My mother would always proclaim that our birth foreshadowed things to come. I came quietly. Jered, who would spend the rest of his life being called Jubby, announced his entrance into the world dramatically by grabbing the hook-like device the doctor used to pull him out. Like Thor with his mythical hammer, the newborn lifted this medical instrument into the air announcing his presence. My mother looked up at him in wonder, hearing the twin cries of babies that would provide a lifetime of adventure.

She left the hospital looking like she had gone a few rounds with Muhammad Ali. Two black eyes looked out of a permanently half-frozen face. Her liver was shot and her kidneys were messed up. Worse, she would have to recover quickly. Now she had the job of going home to take care of two tiny babies, a six-year-old tyrant, and a neurotic husband. She left the hospital a survivor. It had been a traumatizing experience, but everything worked out.

My mother had heeded the doctor's advice and not seen *Jaws* that summer. She would never witness the horror of a great white shark terrorizing innocent swimmers in the ocean. It turned out there was something more terrifying for her to experience, giving birth to a two-headed monster…twins.

Smile, you son of a…boom!

2

"The Twins"

Nicknames are funny. They're truer to our identity than our real names. When I was a kid, I wasn't ever called by the first name my parents gave me. My brother and I were just called "The Twins." We were also called by our nicknames. I was "Beej" and he was "Jubby." Brendan and Jered were names written on the birth certificates, but they were largely unused. Most of the time we were "The Twins."

That was okay. We were like a two headed monster, but our two heads could hardly have been more different. Sure, we had to share almost everything. Birthdays, toys, clothes, bowl haircuts. But that's where the sharing stopped. We had nothing in common. There was not a single thing similar about us. I had brown hair; he was towheaded. I was small. He was bigger. From the get-go he was wild and rambunctious while I was quiet and meek. My natural impulses would be to mind my own business and he wasn't afraid of anyone or anything. I was good at avoiding conflict while he seemed to seek it out. I was a sensitive-thinker type, and he was all action all the time. I viewed the world in shades of grey. He saw everything as black and white. The molds of our personalities were cast from the starting line. We were best friends and worst enemies. It was almost always the two of us against the world; a world that saw us as one being, "The Twins." We had been defined by our circumstance and would spend our childhood using this to our advantage.

As a kid you don't realize how much everything around you has an influence on who you are. Ignorance is bliss, right? I once read an article in *National Geographic* about what shapes us the most in our lives. What are the main factors in forming our personalities? According to the article, it is the impact of having siblings. I agreed.

My older brother, Aran, would be a crucial figure in my development. He was always the archetypal big brother, the person in our world we looked up to the most. He knew what was cool and what wasn't. We always wanted to impress him more than anybody. Six years separated us in age, therefore, we thought he knew everything. For example, he knew which bands were worth listening to and which ones were lame. He loved classic rock, therefore, we did too. Aran's musical taste leaned toward bands like AC/DC, Led Zeppelin, and *KISS*. For me, it was always a struggle to figure out the difference between what was good and what wasn't. If you liked something that others consider "uncool" it could leave you with a sense of shame.

That was what I felt when I was allowed to buy my first record album. It was Michael Jackson's *Thriller*. I couldn't wait to impress Aran with my choice. Everybody loved Michael Jackson in 1982 and was talking about *Thriller*. Somehow, I heard the songs and loved them. *Billie Jean, Beat It, Thriller!!* They were awesome and made me want to dance! I figured I had made a good choice and Aran would be proud of me. I had moved on from *Sesame Street* records and now had my first "cool" album in my little hands. Michael Jackson was looking at me from the cover in his white outfit. He looked amazing. My parents brought me home from the store and the first thing I did was run to Aran's room to show him. I was super excited and wanted my big brother to see the great choice I made. He had to see how "cool" my taste in music was. He looked at it for a second and said one word.

"Gay."

I was crushed and couldn't understand the criticism. I thought it was cool. The world seemed to think it was cool. The guy at the record store thought it was a good choice. But, with one word, my older brother shot it down. Aran was six years older and knew more than me. His word was law, and it must be right. I walked away holding my new record in disappointment. I would only listen to it in secret because my older brother didn't think it was cool. This made me wonder about a lot of things. What was cool? What wasn't cool? How do you know the difference? I had no idea and, little did I know, I'd spend the rest of my childhood trying to figure this out.

Luckily, I had a partner in crime to help me. My relationship with Jubby shaped me more than anything. Like I said, he was my best friend and my worst enemy. We were glued together and never torn apart. We learned to do everything together. He would always learn how to do something about one day before me. He found out how to ride a bike first and the next day I figured it out. He learned how to swim and then, a little later, I would pick it up. It was like that with everything.

When we turned four, we were sent to pre-school. Although I was initially nervous and excited, most of my pre-school days were uneventful. Two memories stand out. I remember some kid trying to kiss a girl behind a bunch of cubbies. What the heck!? They were four. That just confused the four-year-old crap out of me. The most distinct memory, however, was on the very first day. Jubby and I were dropped off and left in our new classroom. It had a scent I would smell my entire life, the first day of school smell. Everyone knows exactly what it is; some kind of combination of industrial cleaning product, glue, construction paper, and disinfectant. Every time I enter a school at the beginning of a school year, I smell that same smell. It takes me back to the first day of pre-school every time. Nostalgia through scent is a magical and powerful phenomenon.

Surrounded by the powerful aroma of school on the first day, Jubby and I met the teacher. "You must be the twins. How cute. You look completely different though."

We hated that. We wanted to look alike. But everybody always pointed out that we didn't. That routine got old real fast.

"Aren't twins supposed to look alike?"

Most of the time we wouldn't answer this. How could you? What do you say to that? The world seemed dead set on responding to us with the same stupid phrase.

"Twins. Really? You don't look alike."

It was a conspiracy. We didn't like it, but we got used to it.

With a toothy smile and an upbeat demeanor our new teacher showed us around. I remember being shy and trying to stay close to Jubby. He didn't seem too bothered by the situation. It was important for me to stay close to him. This was a new experience and I needed him to be next to me. He had become like a protective blanket for me. After a quick tour of the room, we were sent outside to play on the playground while other students shuffled in to meet the teacher and get the same lowdown.

Jubby and I were swinging on the monkey bars when we heard the teacher say something that got our attention.

"Oh, wow, more twins. We have *two* sets in the class. Amazing."

We looked over and saw two identically dressed red-headed, freckly mutant four-year-olds being patted on the head by the teacher.

"Those boys over on the monkey bars are twins too. But they're not real twins like you guys. They don't look alike."

What the hell?

Jubby and I knew we didn't share many similarities. We did, however, share one thing. We had a kind of telepathy. It was like an ability to know what the other was thinking and feeling. I'm not making that up. You could chalk it up as a kind of hyper-sensitive awareness that may have developed in the womb. Maybe it had something to do with that X-ray in utero. Who knows? But in that moment, when we heard the teacher say we weren't real twins our twin sense kicked in. We simultaneously felt hurt and angry. That was our identity. How dare she take it away from us!

The two red-headed boys, just like the twins in *The Shining*, shuffled over to us. They walked exactly like one another and in a kind of slow-motion. As they hovered our way, they just stared straight at us. Their beady little eyes were zeroed in on Jubby and me hanging off the monkey bars. We were seeing double. When they spoke, it was in unison.

"We're real twins. You're not."

Then I saw something I would see time and time again throughout my life. It was an amazing, animalistic, and primal instinct. Jubby had a fighting trigger in him that I've never seen in another human being. Those two freckly faced turds never knew what hit them. It took my four-year-old brother half a second to pop one of the so-called "real twins" in the face and the other in the stomach. I just looked on with my jaw on the floor. Boy could those kids cry.

In seconds, the teacher was on top of the entire situation dragging Jubby off a pile of red-headed freckles. She grabbed me by the ear and put us in an extended time out. For the remainder of the year those two kids stayed the hell away from us. Territory had been marked by a pint-sized alpha-dog establishing his dominance. Such is the law of nature, the prison yard, and pre-school in 1979.

He was always my defender and protector, but Jubby could also be a tormentor. Part of the problem was that I was too attached. Kindergarten was a bit of a rough year for me. It certainly didn't get kicked off on the right foot. The school tried to split us up by putting us in two different classrooms. I found this out on the very first day. Where the hell was the fair warning? It was the very first time I was going to be away from my twin and I knew I wasn't going to survive without him. He was right across the hall, but he might as well have been on the friggin' moon. I had but one course of action to take…throw the biggest conniption fit the world has ever seen. And, let me tell you, I raged against the machine that day. I'm still embarrassed by my five-year-old histrionics. Honestly, I will forever be embarrassed by the memory of this conniption. As an adult, any time I see a psychotic little kid on the floor kicking and screaming throwing a temper tantrum, I flashback to my first day of school. Looking back on it, I'm certain I did psychological damage to my innocent classmates who just wanted to get on with their first day of kindergarten. I didn't give two hoots. All I wanted was to be in the same classroom as my brother who had never left my side.

The tantrum worked its magic. I got my way. The construction paper star with my name on it was taken off the classroom door and thrown away. A cut-out construction paper frog labeled "B-R-E-N-D-A-N" was magically produced out of thin air and placed on *another* door next to the cut-out frog that had Jubby's name on it. Mission accomplished. We were in the same class, and I was happy.

I spent most of kindergarten learning to cope with life. Separating myself from my brother was one of the hardest things to deal with. The teacher told my mother that a funny thing would happen every day during nap hour. I don't remember doing this, but apparently our nap time blankets always had to have one corner touching when we settled down to take our mid-day classroom snooze. Apparently, the connection formed in the womb still determined sub-conscious behavior.

When I got to first grade some things had changed. I didn't depend on Jubby nearly as much and we started making friends with other kids. I was still quiet and kept to myself, so this was harder for me. Jubby, on the other hand, did not struggle. He made friends with a kid named Russell. I don't know how they met, but it was a weird and unholy alliance. Jubby was reckless and rambunctious. Russell was semi-retarded. That's not derogatory. He was semi-retarded.

I immediately didn't like the friendship. I'm sure I was jealous and found myself being excluded. Suddenly, my own twin brother was picking on me and had this Russell kid as his new henchman. That sucked. My world was falling apart. The only way to deal with this was to grab an ass-load of comic books, climb a tree and hide from the world. That's what I did day after day. Escapism in more ways than one provided solace. But Jubby and Russell would always find me, call me names, needle me, and terrorize me. Like I said, it sucked.

One of the major differences between Jubby and me was our anger. Jubby's anger was instinctual and would come out in a flash. I was different. I had a deeper kind of anger. It was like a dormant volcano waiting to erupt. It was because of Russell that I would find out about my anger. It would be the first hulking out experience of many that I would have in my early adolescence. It was a long time coming as I had taken a few months of abuse at the hands of my fraternal twin and his ingrate of a new friend. One day, school ended and I was headed out of the building looking forward to going home to watch *The Dukes of Hazzard.*

There were a lot of great shows on television when I was a kid. I loved few shows more than *The Dukes of Hazzard.* That year I began school armed with a *Dukes* lunchbox. I was proudly carrying this little tin lunch pail with a plastic Daisy Duke mug inside of it when I turned a corner and there was Russell. He had been waiting for me in the hallway. For no reason he pushed me. Jubby was right next to him laughing. He pushed me again and smiled a somewhat almost toothless, inbred grin. Jubby said nothing. He just stood there.

"What er ya gonna do? Baby, baby, baby…"

Russell was mocking me. I'm almost positive he made fun of my lunchbox. That was over the line. Somebody had to stand up for Bo and Luke. Somebody had to defend the honor of Daisy. The volcano was roaring somewhere deep inside of me. It was bubbling to the surface.

Jubby suddenly had a look of shame on his face. Maybe he was realizing he shouldn't be letting his twin be treated this way. One glance at him and the guilt on his face made something happen inside of me. The volcano erupted. An anger came out of me that was uncontrollable.

I swung my *Dukes of Hazzard* lunchbox through the air as hard as any six-year-old has ever swung a lunchbox. Boom! It connected against the side of good ol' Russell's knuckle-dragging noggin. The next thing I saw was this window-licker laying on the ground spastically twitching. Holy Jesus! I killed him. I hovered over him and pointed down at this kid who had been taunting me for months.

"YOU DID THIS! YOU DID THIS! YOU MADE ME DO THIS! THIS IS WHAT YOU GET!"

The next thing that happened was a bit of a blur, but it went something like this: My older brother, Aran, just so happened to be in the vicinity of my hulking out. He grabbed me and together we ran outside to my bike.

"Ride home, buddy. Just ride. Go, go, go, go."

I did. I frantically peddled two blocks with tears streaming down my cheeks and that "ugly cry look" underneath my bowl haircut. I ran to my room, grabbed a bunch of comic books, went out to my tree, climbed up and continued crying. I was convinced I killed Russell.

Eventually my mother's footsteps could be heard approaching the tree.

"I killed him," I sobbed.

"No, you didn't. He's fine. Come down. You're not in trouble."

I came down sobbing every step of the way. She hugged me for a long time. I just couldn't stop crying. I felt betrayed by my brother, but things would get patched up. What really made me cry was the scariness of my own anger… being out of control. Whoa…that was terrifying and something that still scares me as an adult. It's still there. Along with *The Dukes of Hazard,* one of my favorite shows as a kid was *The Incredible Hulk.* Something about a mild-mannered guy erupting into anger and turning into a raging, green monster unnerved me. Somehow, I knew there was an angry Hulk living deep down inside me. I was quiet and shy by nature, but I could feel my own Hulk wanting to get out. This was a feeling that scared me. It was anger. It would take a lot to trigger this fury, but once that fuse was lit, watch out! That day, the Hulk inside me made his first appearance. And poor moronic Russell never saw it coming.

Russell didn't die and he remained friends with Jubby for a few more months. He also warmed up to me after I knocked his ass out. School ended and first grade was over. One day my father wanted to take us to our grandmother's house to go swimming. She had a full-sized swimming pool. My brother asked if Russell could come. Sure. We got to the pool and my father told us to hang out on the deck while he went into the house to talk to my grandmother.

"Don't even think about going in until I get back out here."

As has been established, Russell was not the sharpest tool in the shed, so to speak. Another characteristic was that he was completely unable to swim. The kid couldn't swim a stroke. I'm not sure if he heard what my father had said about not going in the pool or whether Russell just couldn't control himself. Either way, my dad was not there, and Russell decided to jump in the ten-foot-deep end of the pool. He began drowning. Jubby and I could swim. In fact, we were good swimmers. But neither of us knew anything about proper lifesaving techniques. And there we were looking at a boy flailing around in our grandmother's pool. There was no doubt that he was going to drown. In a moment of crisis, questions quickly come to mind. Do we run for help? No. Do we throw him a line? No. Does my impulsive brother jump in after him? Yep.

Jubby to the rescue. Unfortunately, a panic-stricken moron flailing about in the pool proved to be too much for even Jubby. I remained calm. It wasn't my nature to freak out. Standing on the deck looking at two drowning kids, a thought came to me. Don't panic. I looked over and saw the long pole of the pool skimmer. I walked to it, picked it up, turned around and extended it in the direction of the splashing water. My brother was able to grab it and I pulled the two of them to the deck.

After he caught his breath and regained whatever composure he was capable of, Russell said to me, "Yer pretty smart."

"Thanks," I said.

Jubby just looked at me. "Thanks Beej," he said.

We were okay.

3

Playboys

My older brother used to throw sharp knives into my crib when I was a baby. That sounds terrible and I guess it is. In his defense, he was a six-year-old boy who had the run of the roost his entire life. He would always claim that he only wanted one brother so he could have bunk beds. Instead, he got two brothers and no bunk beds. I don't think he was ever doted on in his early years, but whatever attention he was used to getting almost certainly dried up when his twin brothers arrived in his world.

Having survived flying cutlery, Jubby and I would grow up in a constant state of being hazed. Aran seemed to have a genius when it came to purely psychological torture. I really can't remember getting into a physical fight with him. He was six years older and must have been aware that beating up on much smaller kids would look bad. But our presence was an annoyance that had to be dealt with, and he had a nimble mind when it came to ways of handling his underlings. Maybe he was a Nazi interrogator in a former life? I remember seeing a movie called *The Marathon Man*. There is a famous scene in which a sadistic Nazi torturer, tries to get information out of a terrified victim by extracting teeth from his head sans anesthesia. The Nazi, with German accent, pulls tooth after tooth during a long interrogation. The scene totally freaked me out because that was Aran to me when I was a kid…a damned Nazi torturer.

I grew up Catholic. My father was Captain Catholic. He was a proud member of the team and waived the flag as high as anybody. It was crucial to him that the values of the Church be passed on to his sons. This would have an enormous impact on me. I was baptized in the Catholic church and spent every Sunday and every Holy Day of Obligation of my youth there. Church scared me but also gave me a tremendous sense of awe. All that ceremony and tradition is strong juju for a kid. I guess that was the point.

Our priest was a very nice man named Father Francis. He was kind and gentle and deserves no criticism. In fact, he should be anointed a saint for putting up with Jubby and me as altar boys. The nuns, on the other hand, could be demonic, ruler-wielding trolls. Some of them were nice and armed with an unending purse of candy, but others could be scary.

It wasn't overtly the intent, but growing up Catholic produced in me a classic mixture of guilt, anxiety, shame, and fear. It got into the bloodstream early on and hasn't really left me as an adult. Another by-product was that the Church also made me fear demonic possession. That was my worst nightmare. To have an evil spirit inhabiting your corporeal being was way too much for me to handle. I would lay in bed awake at night terrified at the thought of it. It didn't help that when we asked anybody from the clergy, they would tell us that it *was* true and that it could happen. That wasn't the answer I was looking for.

I remember a four-foot-tall Sister Rosemary, during religious education classes, spending a terrifying hour telling us about the time she witnessed an exorcism taking place in frickin' Calcutta. If that wasn't enough to fry the innocence of childhood off you, I don't know what is. Why would a nun lie? Why would the priest spend time telling us about how he was trained in seminary to perform exorcisms? My little brain was fried. Do demons really exist? The devil? Ahhhh!! You can see why I'd be terrified and anxious. Out of desperation, I even stole holy water from the church sponge tray and kept it under my mattress. I needed whatever protection I could get. One night, gripped by fear of the devil, I gulped down my vial of holy water convinced a stomachache might be demonic possession. That was my state of mind very early on. I was afraid of everything, but the thought of demonic possession was a daily terror, and the Church authority was doing nothing to calm my fears.

That is why what my big brother did to me was particularly cruel. I was six and he was twelve. My parents, being clueless about the movies their kids were watching, were unaware that my older brother had somehow seen *A Clockwork Orange*. It certainly wasn't appropriate, but Aran was good at finding things that were forbidden. What a rebel.

After seeing the film, he was inspired. He was particularly impressed with the method of "aversion therapy" the main character is forced to endure. If you've never seen it, a criminal is cured of violent impulses by being strapped to a chair with his eyeballs pinned open. He is unable to shut them as images of violence are played on a movie screen in front of him. Simultaneously he is being given some kind of drug that makes him feel ill while he watches the mayhem on the screen. He would associate illness with violence, and this would cure him of evil impulses. This gave Aran an idea. If it worked in the movie, maybe it would work on his little brother.

Before I knew it, I was tied with rope and bungee cords to a wooden chair. My brother and a sadistic twelve-year-old friend of his were turning me into a very unwilling Harry Houdini. Unfortunately, there would be no escape and there would be a long-lasting impact. Claustrophobia sucks but it doesn't even begin to describe how I felt being tied to the chair that day. This was terrifying. I kicked and screamed myself like a banshee and howled until I was hoarse. My screaming went on for the better part of an hour. I wore myself out and was eventually reduced to an exhausted puddle. It was then that my brother enacted the most insidious part of his plan. He had rented *The Exorcist* movie. I watched as he turned the television on and inserted the most horrifying movie ever made into the VCR. His intention was to give me my own personal form of aversion therapy. The result was an aversion to sleeping alone for the next two months.

If you've never seen *The Exorcist*, let me tell you, it is truly terrifying! It's even more terrifying when you've been told by nuns and priests that it can really happen. Bound and exhausted, I sat for two hours and watched as a little girl became possessed by a demon. I watched her transform from a sweet little girl to a foul and ghastly creature. That look in her eyes. That wicked voice. There should be a label on the movie that reads: NOT FOR A SIX-YEAR-OLD.

The movie ends happily…sort of. The demon is cast out of the girl and the hero saves the day. I, on the other hand, wasn't given a sense of relief. When it was over, I became physically ill. I was given the typical older brother threat not to tell mom and dad, or else. Amazingly, I didn't. But they must have known something was up when I spent the next two months of my life insisting they let me sleep with them. I couldn't get the images out of my head. I couldn't help imagining my bed was shaking and levitating the way it did in the movie. There was no way I could sleep alone. Eventually I would recover from the experience, but the emotional and psychological impact was profound.

The worst hazing, at the hands of my maniacal brother, was far more evil and far more sadistic than forcing a six-year-old to watch a horror movie. It was a very long-term form of torment. It was torture that the CIA, FBI, and KGB would admire. It was deliberate. It was cruel. It may even have bordered on evil. And it happened almost daily for over a decade. It was a dominant part of my childhood, and even followed me into life as an adult. It involved sex, pornography, shame, and blackmail. It's also the reason that when I hear the word "Playboy," a paralyzing feeling of shame washes over me like a cold wave.

I was eight. For some reason my parents were constantly leaving and employing babysitters to watch over Jubby and me. My folks were great in their own quirky way, but they weren't around much of the time. Aran was old enough to watch us, but after realizing the kind of damage he was capable of, my folks decided it might be safer to get a teenage girl to keep us in line. I remember a constant stream of babysitters. They never had much to do with us. For the most part, they'd just sit on the couch and watch television. We were mostly left to our own devices. It was a good set-up, but this situation would also lead to the worst form of torture imaginable.

We grew up in an old farmhouse. It had a very large attic upstairs. It was a long room that had no electricity. There was a broken window at the end of it. The door that opened into it was always closed. Nobody wanted to look into a room that barely had plaster on the walls and was filled with junk from top to bottom. Boxes filled with everything you could imagine were scattered willy-nilly all over the place. There were ancient lamps, old toys, cobwebs, framed portraits of ghostly looking people from another century, a phonograph, and every other imaginable thing you could think of that would fill a creepy, old attic. There was no discernible organization to it. I'm not sure where any of it came from. It was probably a mixture of junk my parents inherited and stuff that was left by the previous owner of the house. The attic was a place that was fascinating and terrifying, but it also held something so provocative that it would yield one of the worst cases of blackmail in human history.

Most days in one's life are uneventful and inconsequential. Every once and awhile there's a day that changes everything. You almost never see these days coming. One fateful Saturday afternoon, my parents were gone. The babysitter was on the couch watching *Solid Gold*. Aran was lurking somewhere. We never really knew when he would pop up. He just came and went as he pleased. Jubby and I had two of our best friends, Patrick and James, over. Out of boredom we decided to invade the attic for treasures and see what we could find. We began rifling through junk and investigating what was inside the mountains of cardboard boxes scattered all over the room. Then it happened. I'm not sure which one of us initially found it, but I do remember what was said. "OH – MY - GOD!"

We all rushed over to peer down into a large cardboard box. It was full of magazines that had the word *Playboy* written at the top. What the hell is a *Playboy*? I'm a boy and I like to play. Is this a magazine for me, then? Each magazine had a woman on the cover staring at you in a way I'd never seen women look before. They were beautiful. I immediately felt *weird*. That is the best word for the moment: *Weird*. There was something *weird* about the way the women on each magazine was dressed or, to be fair, not dressed. The poses were *weird*, and they made me feel *weird*. I felt *weird* but I also felt nervous. Somehow, I knew that what was in these magazines would be forbidden to my very young eyes. Jubby, Patrick, and James knew it too. It didn't matter. Despite the feeling of weirdness, temptation had been ignited and there was no turning back. Our little hands started grabbing at these magazines. Somehow all those women, those sirens, were calling for us to open the pages and find out what was inside.

"Oh. My. God."

"Look at those!"

"What the…"

"Look at this one."

"Those are huge!"

We had hit the jackpot of forbidden knowledge. My heart was racing. This felt so wrong, but the excitement was almost nauseating. We became like rabid, salivating monsters pouring over pages and pages of nudity our eight-year-old minds were not meant to see and certainly couldn't comprehend. We were maniacs. We were pirates who had unearthed buried treasure, and we were rolling around in it. We didn't even know what sex was and we certainly had no idea about female anatomy. We only knew we were excited by it. This was as powerful a force as being possessed by a demon, and we were in its devilish grip. Eight-year-old unleashed horniness. Look out ladies!!

After about an hour studying hundreds of naked female bodies, we were full of an energy we never knew existed. We were no longer ourselves. Our thinking became altered. We *needed* to have these magazines and these women all to ourselves. They had to be stored in *our* territory. Our lives depended on it and we had to make a plan.

"We need to take these to the club house," somebody said.

"Great idea," someone else agreed.

"No, that's the best idea, ever."

We quickly devised the most unprofessional smuggling job that ever took place. Actually, there was no real plan. We were way too horned up to do anything involving logic or reason. The initial idea was for each of us to tuck a couple magazines under our shirts. We were then supposed to head downstairs trying to look cool and collected. The tough part would involve passing by the unwitting babysitter sitting on the couch watching her show. Once this was achieved, we would scurry to the clubhouse and stash the treasure. If everything went according to plan, our stashed treasure of naked women would make us the kings of the universe. We couldn't explain it. All I know is we couldn't control ourselves. Our entire way of life seemed to depend on this mission.

At first, things were going smoothly. The first few trips were successful. You could even hear the *Mission Impossible* theme song in the background somewhere. Everything was great. The plan was working. Then, during one trip, the babysitter asked, "What are you guys doing?"

"Nothing."

This brief exchange made us nervous. Oh, God. The mission was in danger. She suspected something. She knows. Oh, God. What do we do?

But we couldn't stop. We had to keep going. We needed them all.

There was a consensus that we were taking too many trips. The mission was in danger. We decided that it would be best to make a Hail Mary pass. One of us would have to take the entire box, the remainder of the booty…so to speak. Jubby was the strongest, so he was the man for the job. Before we knew it, he had a large box of 1960s and 70s vintage pornography in his eight-year-old arms and was struggling to carry it downstairs. Everything seemed to hang in the balance. He was halfway down the stairs when the box ripped wide open spilling dozens of forbidden nudey magazines across the stairs and onto the landing below. *Holy mother of God!* Tits and ass everywhere!

"What are you guys doing?" the babysitter called.

We panicked.

"Grab them. Pick them up. Hurry."

A mad scurry of terrified floundering took place to scoop up all the shameful evidence from the floor. In seconds we collected them and fumbled our way to the clubhouse to complete our stash.

There was no doubt that the babysitter knew something was going on, but what exactly did she know? Could she have known that, while she was hanging out watching television, a massive sexual awakening was taking place and turning her charges into little porn hoarders? We were in denial, but it would turn out she knew everything. Worse, we would eventually come to find that she would pass her knowledge on to my sadistic older brother. In doing so, our babysitter would unwittingly make our lives a holy hell for years to come.

But, back to the mission. We were in our clubhouse surrounded by mountains of semi-naked women. The mission had not exactly gone to plan. We were flustered. This had turned out to be a terrible idea. Hiding that many nudey mags in the clubhouse was impossible. We were idiots. There was no doubt we were going to get caught. Getting all that porn down to the clubhouse was hard enough. How the hell were we supposed to get them back up to their original home? A heated debate took place. It got ugly. We had become criminals turning on each other. We were feeling some kind of horrible combination of fear, shame, and sexual excitement. All those beautiful naked ladies were to blame for making us lose control of ourselves. I'd felt a lot of things, but I'd never felt anything like this. I had been afraid before but nothing like this. Shame is a sickening feeling and the four of us were being emotionally torn apart by it.

To add fuel to the fire, my parents suddenly returned. We could see the car pulling into the driveway. The sight of our parents made us frantic. We were little criminals holed up like Ned Kelly in the clubhouse. What were we going to do? There was absolutely no way we could get all those naked women back in the attic now. Desperation set in.

"Let's bury them."

I don't know who said it, but everyone quickly agreed that we had to do it. It was the only way that we could avoid being caught.

Suddenly we were all carrying shovels and headed into the back woods resting thirty yards from the back of the clubhouse. With panic in our hearts, we frantically began to dig a grave for our beautiful, naked women. Our digging was frantic, and dirt was flying everywhere. We were digging maniacs fueled by unspent sexual energy and fear. We couldn't explain it. We knew only one thing. The objects that had created our foolishness and turned us into horny little demons must be hidden forever. If caught, we couldn't begin to imagine what the punishment would be.

Two hours had passed since we first stumbled upon that horrible box. Much had changed within us. A threshold had been crossed. This was unchartered territory. Now the box and all its original contents were thrown into a hastily dug hole in the ground and covered up. The job was done. We were sweaty, dirty, and exhausted but we sighed with relief. A bullet had been dodged. We had avoided the unknown consequence of getting caught looking at boobs and pubic hair…or, so we thought.

Aran, with a devilish grin, entered our bedroom. Oh, no! I knew that look. It wasn't good. I started sweating. My mouth became dry as panic paralyzed me. My big brother had the same look in his eye right before forcing me to watch *The Exorcist*. This was going to be the beginning of years of torture. We just knew it. This was something we would have to live with for a long time. He had something on us, and he was going to use it.

He sat on my bed and looked at us gleefully. He whispered one terrible word, "Playboys." That's it. That's all he said. Hell, that's all he had to say. The simplicity was brilliant. This was knowledge and knowledge was power. Somehow, he knew that saying just that one word would allow him to control us. At that moment, there were no two syllables more terrifying than the ones he just said. He didn't say anything else. Aran just turned around and left.

Oh my God. He knew. He knew. How could he know? The babysitter. *Oh my God.* He's gonna tell Mom and Dad. He's gonna tell Mom and Dad. What are we gonna do?

Here's the thing: He never actually did tell my parents about our brief encounter with Hugh Hefner's life's work. Why would he? If he told, he would have lost his power. Over the years he would be guilty of conducting more blackmail than anyone in the history of the world. He only needed to use one terrible word and he used it to his fullest capabilities.

Whenever he wanted to make us do one of his chores, whenever he wanted to threaten us, whenever we were bothering him, whenever we looked at him sideways, whenever he was too lazy to get up and get something for himself, he would raise his voice into a girlish soprano and singsong the one word that would get us to do his bidding. "Plaaaayybooooys!" I'll give him credit; he maximized every ounce of his control over us. Like a super-villain in a James Bond movie, he must have had some kind of deep understanding of the power of sexual adolescent shame. Aran's talent was in torment. He truly had a devious mind, and he lorded his authority over us for years. Just seeing him get the glint in his eye and begin the word "Pla…" would send us into hysterics and we would become slaves groveling before their master.

"We'll do anything for you…just please don't tell. Please, please, please." It was pathetic. We were helpless victims of our sexual crime, our lust, our weakness of the flesh, our secret shame. And that's how we came to exist. This was our new normal. We lived in fear and in shame for the rest of our adolescence. Blackmail hung over us like a dark cloud. We spent almost every day of our youth at a constant DEFCON NINE.

Many years later, Jubby and I found ourselves in a room full of family and friends. We were in our twenties, and both established as adults. The occasion was to honor my brother for a milestone birthday or something. After a few beers we decided it would be a good idea to deliver an impromptu speech as a tribute. In the process we decided to come clean about our eight-year-old perversions with the *Playboys*. We thought it would be time to get the monkey off our backs. To do so publicly and officially seemed appropriate. In good jest we would let the world know how evil Aran had been to us growing up.

In retrospect, we came to appreciate our older brother with fondness. As siblings grow older, for better or worse, they gain a sense of appreciation for one another. Big brothers toughen you up. It's their job. Aran was good at it; one of the best. So, we told the story of the *Playboys* to a room full of people, the same story I have written here. They were in hysterics. Aran laughed the hardest. He knew we appreciated him.

When the story was over somebody in the audience piped up and yelled to my father, "Hey, Billy, why'd you have all that porn back then?"

"Those were going to be worth money," he responded.

Maybe the entire incident saved my father from being arrested for selling black-market pornography. Silver linings.

Aran was more than a tormentor and he was more than a big brother. He was always the arbiter of cool things and his opinions always mattered. He did what all big brothers are supposed to do. He helped prepare us for the ways of the world. It might not have been intentional, but it did the job. Jubby and I would be grateful…eventually. The three of us were brothers who learned from one another. Every day was full of shenanigans that leave you dazed and confused. That's brotherhood.

But the one thing I know, without the shadow of a doubt, is that the word "Playboys" still sends a shiver down my spine.

4

Concussed!

Embarrassment is something you never forget. The mortification of doing something stupid stays with you forever. How awful is that occasional moment where a memory of something embarrassing randomly taps you on the shoulder of your brain to remind you how much of an idiot you can be? Embarrassment never really leaves you. It just hides inside and comes out every once and awhile to check your ego. I'll never forget the time I fell, not down, but up the stairs as a group of cute girls were behind me. I will always be haunted by how it felt when I gave a speech in front of my entire high school debate class only to realize my zipper was down the entire time. I remember being in third grade and sneezing a ridiculous load of snot directly into my hand and having an entire group of classmates look over to see me unsuccessfully trying to hide it. "Ewe, you're gross." Oh, the shame! Those memories are never forgotten, but more than that, the feelings attached to them torment us into adulthood.

In movies, people get flashbacks when they experience something that reminds them of their past. As stupid as it might sound, the sight of a kid riding a bike and wearing a helmet sends me into one of those movie-like flashbacks. It's an image that reminds me of the unique pain of embarrassment attached to the trauma of childhood.

The 1980s were not terribly concerned with the safety of kids. Not too many people wore helmets when riding a bike. Now, it's written into law that you need to wear some kind of head-gear if saddling up on a BMX. Back then, times and attitudes were different. A lot of things were considered cool: Pinch-rolled jeans, gigantic hair requiring enough Aqua-net to destroy the ozone layer, *Miami Vice,* and neon colors fell into the category of being rad. On the other hand, wearing a helmet was not cool and was not done by anyone, anywhere…except me.

Trust me, it wasn't by choice that I found myself having to wear some kind of cranial protection throughout my childhood. Whenever I rode a bike or had to do anything that might involve a head injury, my parents would call out, "Don't forget your helmet." None of my friends had this problem. Every one of them gave me a massive amount of crap, too. Yep. It turns out that wearing a helmet was a sure-fired way to guarantee the scorn and ridicule of your peers every time you were made to strap it on. Looking back, nothing good came of it. I didn't even get a cool nickname like "Crash" or something. Nope, not with my friends. They called me "Paper Head." I didn't have a witty comeback. Why try? There isn't a heck of a lot of defense you can muster when you're a scrawny eight-year-old wearing a massive oversized plastic bubble around your noggin.

That's the real kicker. The helmet I wore wasn't even like one of the nifty aerodynamic bike helmets that would be worn in later years. I don't even think those existed back then. No, I had to wear what my parents must have bought in some crappy Salvation Army somewhere. It was a giant, white, Bauer hockey helmet. You could see this thing coming a mile away, like a Thanksgiving Day Parade balloon sailing through the streets of town.

I looked like a Bobblehead and felt tremendously self-conscious. The notion of being the least cool kid in your gang of bike-riding friends was deeply ingrained in my fragile adolescent psyche. You're acutely aware that from an outsider's point of view, the dreaded helmet made you look like the "special" kid in the group. You just know everyone feels sorry for you and assumes your friends only include you because their moms told them to. I would imagine the conversations of the adults sitting on their porches watching us ride around town.

"Doug, why does that boy wear that big, white helmet?"

"You mean 'Paper Head' Heaney? Well, Nancy, I think the boy is mentally retarded."

"That poor boy. How nice that those other boys include him."

The story behind the helmet's existence goes back to an incident that would mark the beginning of a lifetime of injuries. I was forced to wear this monstrosity because of an accident when I was five. That's when I had my first concussion. By the time I was eight, I had logged three other concussions. That was enough to turn me into "Paper Head Heaney." Eventually I would log a grand total of *nine* concussions. That's a lot, even by NFL standards. Should nine concussions be concerning? I've never been too worried and I'm weirdly proud of them. It's both a badge of honor and a source of deep embarrassment. This is the kind of thing that is both complicated and contradictory about life. Sometimes people get competitive about the dumbest things. We compare and measure ourselves against others. Physical injuries are one of those things.

Who suffered the worst injury? Who has the biggest scar? Who came closest to dying by doing something stupid? People are strange. But, in those conversations, I get to brag about nine concussions. We can be proud of the weirdest things, but I get it. Your scars and wounds are part of your identity. They're a reminder of experiences that shape you. Also, they can come in handy as a valid excuse for any boneheaded thing you do.

"Honey, you went to the store and forgot to get the milk."

"Oops…Damn concussions."

"Mr. Heaney, did you grade our tests yet?"

"Ooops…Damn concussions."

"Daddy, why are you driving the wrong way down a one-way street."

"Ooops…. Damn concussions."

Most of my head injuries came from playing sports, general recklessness, or being in the wrong place at the wrong time. My first concussion, and by far the worst, came from a lack of appreciation for physics. If only Mrs. Moore had taught me the formula to calculate the coefficient of friction back in kindergarten, I wouldn't have suffered so many cranial mishaps.

It was when I was in kindergarten that I suffered my first, and by far the worst, concussion of my life. My parents, looking to beat the inevitable cabin fever of the harsh winter months, had a great idea. They thought it would be nice to take advantage of the extreme cold and create an ice-skating rink in our side yard. This would work perfectly to entertain their three energetic sons for weeks. We went out in the freezing cold, bundled up like Eskimos, and cleared out the snow for a circular ice rink. A three-foot tall snowbank was built around a circular shaped clearing. The garden hose provided water that very quickly turned into a sheet of ice. Let the skating commence!

I remember strapping on a pair of ice-skates for the first time. They were trainer skates. Instead of one blade, there were two that were an inch apart on each skate. This would make things easier for a five-year-old who had never been on ice before. Inside the house, my mother tied the skates onto my feet. My brothers were skated up as well. It was super exciting to do anything outside the house. We had been cramped up in the house for too long and needed to get out. I remember feeling like I couldn't wait to get on that rink and skate around. We had been watching ice skating on the television for weeks. The 1980 Winter Olympics had been on television, and my naïve kindergarten brain was occupied with the thought that I'd magically be able to get on the ice and do triple axels and spins and all the other amazing things Olympic skaters were doing. Tragically, this would not come to any fruition…ever.

With chilly breath coming out of our mouths, my brothers and I stood at the top of the three-foot-high bank looking down at the mirror of ice we had created. My father commanded us to wait on the snowbank and not start skating until he came outside to supervise us. My excitement was too much. I couldn't wait. First, I was cold and wanted to move. But mostly I wanted to prove I had the same talents as the Olympians I had been watching on television. I wasn't very realistic as a five-year-old.

I remember jumping off the snowbank and watching my trainer skates hitting the ice. I remember slipping backwards and the final thing I saw were grey clouds spinning backwards against a blue sky. Then came darkness. And then I remember waking up.

I was not outside anymore. I was inside our living room. The TV was blaring *The Muppet Show*. Fozzy the Bear was yelling "Wakka, Wakka, Wakka." My eyes opened to a familiar world, but everything was wrong. The room was spinning around me uncontrollably. My head felt like it was going to explode. Everything hurt. Thinking hurt. Breathing hurt. Crying hurt. I had no idea how I had gotten from the ice-rink to the couch. I didn't know how much time had passed. I barely knew who I was.

Blechhhhhh! I immediately threw up everywhere. My head ached and the room was spinning. Blechhhhh! I puked again. All I wanted to do was fall asleep and I wasn't allowed. People didn't rush kids to the emergency room back then…at least my parents didn't. Even though their child had knocked himself completely unconscious, their panic level only reached the point of calling a doctor over the phone. He told them I most likely had a concussion, and they shouldn't let me fall asleep as this might result in me not waking up ever again. I learned about dry-heaves and vertigo. It was the first of many times throughout my life where the pain of living was such that, although I've never been even close to suicidal, I truly at that moment would have embraced death.

Sometimes moments from our childhood are oddly familiar when we become adults. It's the déjà vu phenomenon we all know about. The first night I spent in college was the first time I ever got black-out drunk. To be fair, I had no idea what I was doing and was beyond unprepared. However, when I woke up in the morning in my dorm room surrounded by my own vomit and trying to remember what the hell had happened the night before, I made an immediate psychic connection to being five years old and feeling the same way.

What does a bad concussion feel like? Here's what you do to approximate the situation: Drink lots of alcohol for a few hours until you pass out. Then wake up. It's as simple as that. If you follow those few steps, you will know exactly what a concussion feels like. The world will be spinning, your head will feel like it is going to explode, and you'll probably throw up a lot. Little did I know that when I was five, and suffering the effects of a concussion, I'd be having roughly the same feelings thirteen years later. I can't recommend either experience. Head trauma and binge drinking are two things that earned wisdom has taught me to avoid in my more mature years.

For those interested in keeping score, I've included the order and the cause of all nine concussions. Believe me, I'm not bragging.

1. Fell on ice rink.
2. Fell off a cow.
3. Bucked off a horse.
4. Bucked off another horse.
5. Fell on icy sidewalk.
6. Bounced my head off a basketball court.
7. Bounced my head off a soccer field.
8. Hit in the head while boxing.
9. Hit a windshield in a car accident.

There's nothing good about getting a head injury. It's scary. It's agonizing. It seems to last forever, and recovery is a real pain. It can also be life-threatening. I'm told long-lasting neurological problems can be a result. A concussion is uncomfortable and sucks in almost every way. But if I had a choice, I'd rather suffer nine more concussion than wear that god-damned hockey helmet ever again.

5

Getting the Gay Beat Out of Me

As far as I can remember I was spanked exactly twice when I was a kid and both times occurred on the same day. Second grade proved to be one of those pivotal years for me. I continued to be shy and had cemented my place within my family as "the quiet one." I was the George Harrison of the clan. Jubby was the hyper-active one. My mother, Eva, was the glue that held the family together. My father, Billy, was mercurial. He'd be fun one moment and dark another. You never knew what the day would bring. As the big brother, Aran remained somewhat of a tormentor, but as we got older, he delighted in being a comedian with his wicked sense of humor. He would shine particularly well at dinner time, especially on hot dog night when he would wait until my parents weren't looking and place a half-eaten hot dog with ketchup slathered on it in his unzipped jeans. Obviously, this would create the illusion of a boy with a severed penis. Classy, right? While my oblivious parents were still unaware, he would get me and Jubby to look below the table at his clever little magic trick and get us rolling on the ground in hysterics. Milk shot out of my nose on many occasions. The entire family all knew their places, and the roles were dutifully played.

Until second grade my backside had not been threatened from being spanked. To say I was a very mild-mannered kid would be an understatement. I minded my business and was terrified at the idea of getting into trouble. My father only had one rule with us and that was not to swim in the river behind our house. He said he'd whip us if we were ever caught taking a swim there. Furthermore, he went on to tell us stories of how the dangerous currents of the river had claimed hundreds of naughty children just like us. He'd tell an obviously fabricated and elaborate story about a boy who went down to the river to catch some fish and ended up getting caught in the current and drowned a terrible death. Usually, the story was over the top and operated on one agenda: To scare the crap out of us enough to know that the river was forbidden. It was typical fatherly propaganda and it worked. I was sufficiently afraid, and I didn't want to get spanked.

This fear would soon become a reality when I was in second grade. My teacher was a very nice woman named Mrs. Moon. She was a warm person and a good teacher. At least that was my first impression of her. One day my initial feelings proved to be wrong when Mrs. Moon would give me the first spanking of my life. When the day was over, I would be left wondering how such a seemingly friendly and loving teacher could do what she did to me. Especially when I was just minding my own business.

When you're in elementary school you do a lot of lining up to go from one place to another. You line up to go everywhere. Little kids rarely travel anywhere in the school by themselves. One day, our class was lining up to return to our classroom from the school library. We marched in single file looking forward to getting back to some story hour with Mrs. Moon. I had no premonition that what would happen next would end up being a defining moment; a moment of bewildering shame and confusion that would remain monumental in my mind for years to come. Patrick Flynn was my best friend. We happened to be at the front of the line leaving the library and we were the first ones to arrive in the classroom. We immediately went to our desks located at the front of the room.

A new girl to our class was right behind us. Her name was Heather. She came to our school a few weeks before and it was obvious something was not right about her. She had a wild look in her eyes. When you're a little kid, you sense these things. She wasn't normal, so we instinctively tried to stay away from her. Darwinian law could be applied to second grade behavior. I was only seven but I knew this girl was bad news. Little did I know that, because of Heather, trouble was right around the corner waiting with a yardstick.

This is a true story, and in a court of law I will swear an oath on a Bible, God, and my dead grandmothers' honor. Patrick and I are quietly at our desks. The rest of the class is still filling the room. Mrs. Moon, my sweetheart of a teacher, has not yet reached the classroom and is still at the end of the hallway. Crazy-eyed Heather decides, for no good reason, that this would be the moment she would jump on top of her desk and begin doing some kind of exotic dance that wasn't age appropriate for her second-grade classmates. It was basically a strip routine. Imagine something you might see in a seedy bar in Las Vegas. As her dress flew over her head, Patrick and I sat with bewildered expressions on our faces. What the hell was going on? Our eight-year-old eyes had never seen anything like this.

It was then that a ghost from the past came back to haunt me like I was Ebeneezer damned Scrooge. My old friend, simple-minded Russell, was the last to enter the classroom before the teacher. He took one look at the erotic dance Heather was performing on top of her desk and lost his mind. "THEY'RE ALL STRIPPING!!" Those were the three words that came out of Russell's mouth. They came out as if through a megaphone. He yelled it. He yelled it to the classroom and then he turned and aimed the same words down the hallway at Mrs. Moon. "THEY'RE ALL STRIPPING!!"

Suddenly, Mrs. Moon was in the room. Only minutes before my teacher appeared to be a sweet, caring woman; now she had a "take no prisoners" look I had yet to see during that school year. A transformation had taken place and now she gave off the impression of a prison guard who just entered a cell looking to crack some skulls.

Patrick and I had just been sitting in our seats that, as cruel fate would have it, happened to be right next to little Ms. Flashdance's desk. The only thing I can think of is that, for some reason, Mrs. Moon looked at a partially undressed girl and then down at Patrick and me. She must have seen an expression on our faces that must have looked something like guilt. She jumped to a terrible and misguided conclusion of some sort. The only thing we were guilty of was being in the wrong place at the wrong time.

We would come to find that in the court of law that was Mrs. Moon's classroom, you did not get a trial. One did not get any defense, whatsoever. The defendants would be proclaimed guilty by the accusation of a complete halfwit named Russell. Also, keep in mind, the accuser was the same person who had been knocked out by one of the defendants and his trusty lunchbox just a few years prior to this. Furthermore, it was not lost on me that if I hadn't saved good old Russell from drowning in my grandmother's pool, none of the following events would ever have taken place.

"EVERYONE. SIT. DOWN!!"

I'd never heard Mrs. Moon yell until this moment. Everyone sat, even half-naked Heather. Mrs. Moon had reached the front of the classroom and was looking straight down at Heather, Patrick, and me. Something seemed very wrong, and I immediately started to feel a sense of panic. The panic increased when I heard her next words.

"How dare you three do that. I'm ashamed of you."

Do what? What the hell did me and Patrick do? I knew what Heather did, but I had no part in that nonsense.

"But we were just sitting dow…"

"STOP TALKING!"

Silence. The so-called pin everyone talks about could be heard dropping. I felt tears welling up in my eyes and fear was turning my stomach into knots. I didn't understand what was going on. One moment I'm sitting at my desk watching some insane girl taking her clothes off and now I'm being accused of…I'm not sure what I'm being accused of, but the teacher was going ballistic about whatever it was. I looked over at Patrick who looked just like I felt. An injustice was happening. We had been found guilty, not only of a crime we didn't commit, but we didn't even know what the offense was.

"I want the three of you to stand up in front of the class to face your punishment."

Punishment? For what? What did we do?

This was when a yardstick materialized in Mrs. Moon's hands and that's the moment I lost it. Like a baby, I started bawling. It was very apparent what she intended to do. She was going to beat my ass with that yardstick. I'm not sure when corporal punishment ended by decree of law, but it certainly was sometime after this moment. Just my luck.

Heather, the real criminal, was first. She was told to turn her backside to the class, bend over, and grab hold of her ankles. She took the five whacks with glee and giggled through each one. This little psychopath found this funny. Heather had obviously was no stranger to being spanked in the ass. On the other hand, this had never happened to me, and I had become a weeping puddle. I'm sure my crying got worse after every blow I witnessed Heather suffer. I knew I would be facing the same fate within a few minutes. There would be no escape.

Patrick was next. He was not crying as much as I was, but he wasn't exactly doing okay. He took the five swats as well, but he certainly wasn't laughing, he was in pain. Mrs. Moon looked like "Hammering" Hank Aaron at the plate knocking 400-foot dingers. She was hitting my best friend's ass so hard he was moving forward with each blow. Whap! Ahhhhhhh! Whap! Ahhhhh! Patrick ended up standing approximately five inches from where he was when his beating began.

Then it was my turn. I wish I could say I was able to pull myself together and gain some composure. But, no, the horror of the moment would not allow such a thing…not by a long shot.

"Why….ugggggghhhh…..are…….ugggghhhh……you…….doing………this…….to……ugghhh…..me……..?" I sobbed.

"Turn around and bend over."

I turned around slowly, with an ugly-cry face, and heaving chest sobs.

"Grab your ankles!"

I didn't. Bent over, I covered my butt cheeks with both hands. I'd never been spanked and lived in mortal terror of such a punishment. I certainly didn't wake up that morning thinking I was going to school to be assaulted by a yardstick. I had no control over anything and the only thing I could think of doing was protect my hind-end from being smashed into bits by my teacher.

"Move your hands or I'll hit them."

"Nooooo!!"

Whap!

"Ahhhhhhhh! MY FINGERS!!!"

"Move your hands or they'll get hit again."

I removed my shaking and now bruised hands.

Whap!

"Ahhhhhhhhh!"

Whap! Whap! Whap!

"Ahhhhhhhhh!"

I had been brought to my knees. I looked up to see the horrified look of an entire classroom of my peers who had just witnessed some kind of serious medieval torture. Second-grade jaws were on the floor. The looks on their faces told me they felt sorry for me, but they also said one thing very clearly, "Better you than me, man."

"Back to your desks," Mrs. Moon said as she placed the instrument of measurement and child abuse on her desk next to her ceramic Garfield doll.

I delicately sat down with tears flowing from my eyes. Sitting hurt. I felt tender in every way imaginable. I had been violated. I couldn't look at anybody. The shame was too great. I could only stare at the surface of my desk. Taped to the top of it was a laminated piece of construction paper with my name on it. It was in the shape of a star. Underneath my name, Mrs. Moon had written "YOU'RE A SHOOTING STAR!" I sure didn't feel like a star now.

"You can sit with your head down for the rest of the day. Think about what you've done."

I buried my face into my folded arms as my sobbing continued. I was ashamed of myself, and I had no idea why. What had I done? I'd never been more confused and pitiful.

The school day finally ended, and I trudged home crying all the way. I didn't want to talk to anybody. I felt sick. My worst fear was that Mrs. Moon would tell my parents. But what would she tell them? What did I do that was wrong? I really didn't know. I must have done something wrong. Why else would Mrs. Moon hit me with a yardstick? I really couldn't figure this out. There wasn't anything to figure out. An injustice had occurred, and I had been wronged, but I was so confused and scared that I had lost the capacity to understand any of it. A lawyer would have come in handy.

I went to my bedroom to seek refuge inside the comfort of my bed. I don't know how long I laid underneath my *Empire Strikes Back* comforter before I heard the door open and footsteps approaching. The covers were yanked off me.

"Get out of bed."

It was my father. He didn't sound angry. It was worse. He sounded disappointed.

"I heard about what you did in school."

"I don't know what I did," I said with tears dripping out of my eyes.

It was then that I noticed he had a belt in his hands.

"What's that for?"

I was becoming hysterical and beginning to hyperventilate.

"This is to teach you not to do it again."

"Do what?"

I didn't get the answer that day. In fact, I didn't get the answer for a long time. I took the second and final spanking of my life in that moment. It wasn't pretty. I held up about as well as I did in the classroom. First, the ruler. A few hours later, the belt. At least my father didn't punish me in front of an audience. Worse, this was all for some unknown crime adults were telling me I was guilty of but wouldn't specify exactly what it was. They just said that I should have known better and should never do it again. And the punishments didn't stop at the repeated ass beatings. My parents also laid down the law by banning me from watching my favorite television shows for an entire month. No *Dukes of Hazard*, no *Incredible Hulk*, no *CHIPS*. Now it wasn't just child abuse, it was cruel and unusual punishment.

Patrick and I would grow up never talking about what happened. We were too ashamed to bring it up. He had faced a similar experience to mine when his folks confronted him. Apparently, our parents had gotten together and decided to use the same punishment playbook. This event would traumatize us into a long silence. The shame I felt was so deep that I blocked it from my thinking for years.

They say time heals all wounds and I think that's mostly true. Time went by and our psychic wounds didn't exactly heal so much as get pushed out of our conscious thoughts. After it was over, nobody ever brought up the incident. The shame of it was buried deep down and it sat there for a long time, years. Regardless, the unanswered question remained in both of our minds. What the hell did we do?

When Patrick and I grew older, we found ourselves hanging out in my parents' kitchen. We were drinking a few beers and lots of family and friends were around. It was a fun and loose atmosphere. We were all laughing and having a good time reminiscing about the past. I don't know how the topic of the second-grade ass beatings came up, but it did. Emboldened by social lubricant, we finally re-hashed the entire incident. It was cathartic. Our shared shame was being released. This was truly the first time we'd ever confronted the issue. The incident had been unmentionable for so long and now it was being addressed. We sipped our beers and laughed as we found ourselves coming to terms with the event. Of course, there remained the important question. What had we been accused of doing? We turned to my parents.

"Do you guys remember when we got in trouble in second grade?"

"Oh, yeah, that."

"Why did you spank me with a belt? What did Mrs. Moon say we did?"

My father grinned and said, "She told us you guys were *fagging off.*"

And that's how I had the gay beat out of me.

How progressive!

6

The Great Pike Street Feud

Feuds are a funny thing. They've always been part of life. I remember being fascinated by the Capulets and Montagues in *Romeo and Juliet*. Why did those two families not get along? What caused it? Nobody seemed to know. I remember watching *West Side Story* and reading *The Outsiders* when I was a kid. They were all the same stories about people who just couldn't seem to get along. Somewhere you can hear Rodney King's plea echoing for all human history, "Why can't we all just get along?"

But the famous feud between the Hatfields and McCoys fascinated me most. Something about two clans of grizzled rednecks killing each other grabbed my imagination. Maybe it was because I had experienced a long, violent feud of my own. It's my opinion that all these feuds were nothing compared to a much lesser-known conflict that took place in my neighborhood when I was a kid. In fact, if historians ever decided to compare the Hatfield-McCoy feud to The Great Pike Street Feud, they would realize that those old rednecks were total amateurs.

I grew up on a dead-end road that had been named Pike Street well before I ever came to live there. The street only had six houses on it. The neighborhood was both part of a very small town and a bit adjacent to it. We could walk to Main Street stores within a minute, but we were also right next to a vast wooded area that, even though we didn't own the land, was definitely *ours*. We simply called it "The Woods."

The end of our backyard was met with a steep bank descending into an absolute wonderland. The bank was populated by the thickest and most daunting weed I've ever seen. My mother was a gardening fiend and said it was called Japanese Bamboo. She cursed it. Apparently, it was one son-of-a-bitch of a weed to remove. She waged war on it for years and eventually emerged victorious. But before that conquest, the Japanese Bamboo lived heartily as a barrier that descended a fifty-foot slope where it promptly ended as the land flattened out into a beautiful forest. If you looked to the right, you'd see a rickety farm fence that separated the forest from a wide-open pasture. This field occasionally had cows and horses in it. Straight ahead were acres of uncivilized forest. All this geography lay right behind my house. Once you crossed the bamboo and entered the forest you were in a different world enchanted with possibility. It was full of adventure and wonder and we explored every inch of it from the beginning all the way to the end where it eventually was cut off by the river. In these woods, we would use every shred of our imaginations. Some days we would be Indiana Jones and on others we'd be Jedi Knights. One thing was for sure; these were *our* woods, and we would defend them at all costs. It was our kingdom.

The house right next door to my parents had been vacant for a little while. The young couple who lived there had moved out. Being naïve to the danger that a small, vacant house could be bought for a low cost, I initially didn't understand the anxiety my father was feeling.

"Some *scumbags* will probably buy it," I heard him kept saying.

"What's a scumbag Dad?" I asked.

I can't remember how my father answered but it didn't matter. I was soon to find out because he was right. The dreaded scumbags would, in fact, buy it.

The Wingers moved in, and our peaceful neighborhood would never be the same. We didn't know it then, but it was the dawn of a new era. Pike Street *had* been an idyllic place. It was quaint and calm. Imagine Norman Rockwell being commissioned by *The Saturday Evening Post* to paint a place that defined small town American values and you have a picture of the neighborhood where I grew up. Maple trees lined the street and created a kind of cove. It was a small road that led nowhere. Birds seemed to sing in praise of it year-round and the inhabitants of this address felt immune to the problems of the larger world outside. That's the kind of place it was. But it had come to an end. A feud was on the horizon.

The war began almost immediately. At eight years old I wasn't prepared for the likes of the Wingers. Bryce was the patriarch. He was a scrawny truck-driver who spent most of his time on the road driving his "big rig" across the country. His wife was Crystal. She was scrawnier than he was and had jet black hair. A cigarette always hung from her mouth. If I'd known what a heroin addict was when I was eight, I would have guessed that she was a junkie but, being ignorant of such things, I just thought she looked like an angry skeleton. She was the first person I ever saw who could do that thing where you put your fingers in your mouth to make a super-loud whistle. It would be used daily and echo throughout the neighborhood to call her children to the house.

There were three children. The youngest was a two-year-old toddler named Sweet-Pea who usually could be found sitting in a mud-puddle in the middle of the road wearing only a soiled diaper. That baby loved mud puddles. When cars came down the street, they just drove around her. Jackson was the next up. He was slightly younger than we were and resembled a feral child because he was always dirty and had a dead look in his eyes. However, where a feral child has natural cunning and cleverness, Jackson was as dumb as a box of doorknobs. Carl was the oldest. He was maybe a year younger than we were. He was a pure criminal. He wasn't dumb like Jackson. The look in his eye was crafty. He seemed like he was always scouting things out – just looking for things to steal. He was the kind of kid you just knew would end up in jail someday. His presence immediately inspired my parents to begin locking the house tighter than Fort Knox.

It would prove not to matter. It didn't take long before Carl and Jackson would be causing chaos up and down the street. The first offenses were small and seemed insignificant. They'd ride their bikes in our yard and leave their toys scattered throughout the neighborhood. Those might seem like minor annoyances to most, but not to Jubby and me. Our hackles were up. We didn't like the situation from the get-go. The neighborhood would need defense and we felt the burden of responsibility. This was real territorial pissing stuff. Millions of years of evolution hadn't changed anything. We would become like the tribes of pre-evolved ape-men in *2001* fighting over a water hole.

Sensing that tension was growing, my parents sat Jubby and me down at the kitchen table. My mother told us to take "the high road" and try to get along. Even at nine years old, our instincts told us this was an impossibility. There was no "high road" with scumbags. My father knew this too, but his concern carried an agenda along with it. He wanted us to be vigilant and defend the neighborhood. Mostly he didn't want our house to be vandalized and thought his own sons could do a decent job of keeping things together. However, he had a stern warning to us, and he was dead serious about it.

"Do you know what it means to be sued?" He asked us.

"Nope."

"Well, being sued is when scumbags like the Wingers take you to court and try to take all your money."

"How do they do that, Dad?"

"Lots of ways."

"Like what?"

"They'll sue you if you lay a finger on them."

My old man looked straight at us with a sober expression on his face. Even though this speech was being given to both of us, I knew it was mostly directed at Jubby. We all knew it would only be a matter of time before the two new inhabitants of Pike Street would get the ever-living crap kicked out of them by my impulsive twin brother.

"Neither one of you is allowed to get into a fight with them. If you do, we'll be sued. They'll take our house, our cars, our clothes, our food, and your toys. We'll be homeless and it'll be because you guys got into a fight with scumbags. That's what scumbags do. They sue you and take all your money."

Wow. Scumbags sucked. Got it.

We left the little family meeting a little wiser but also puzzled. It was going to be hard to turn the other cheek. For Jubby, this directive might have been too much to ask. We didn't know exactly what it meant to take the high road. The only thing we really knew was that Carl and Jackson were the type of kids who were going to start some drama and we weren't allowed to lay a finger on them.

Slowly but surely the offenses became worse. Carl and Jackson stole out of my parents' garage, they vandalized our clubhouse, and they'd yell all sorts of nasty things at us. The insults that came out of their illiterate mouths were comical. Phrases like "Shit-bandit, assface, and cock-knocker" became as common in the neighborhood as the birds singing. I'm sure, as is always the case, the vocabulary of their parents was the root of their colorful taunts.

In general, their overall presence cast a very dark cloud over what was once a peaceful street. We had been invaded and, worse than anything, we were not allowed to do anything about it. Or at least, we'd been told not to fight. It turned out that was okay. Fighting would have been for amateurs. We would discover other ways to deal with the situation. We would have to be imaginative. The war would be long, but we were up to the task. In a way, having a somewhat sadistic older brother in our formative years had prepared us in the same way that a drill-sergeant prepares soldiers in boot camp. We had learned from the best.

The first thing we did was to find their weakness. It was obvious to Carl and Jackson that Jubby and I always had something going on. Our house was the main destination for our crew and our group of buddies were perpetually coming over to hang out. We'd play football or wiffle ball in the side yard almost every day. We were a gang that looked like something you would want to join if you were another kid.

"Can we join your club?" This was the question that came from our new neighbors.

They'd already proven that they were not to be trusted and we certainly didn't like them. No, let me amend that, we despised them. These were not your ordinary misunderstood kids. They were criminals. If they had been nice kids, we would have responded differently, but our immediate answer to their question was a definite "no." Of course, being rejected only incited more criminality in them. Their response was to retaliate by being more destructive, causing more vandalism, and acting even more obnoxious towards us. We began seeing tools and other items from our garage laying around in their yard. The insults became more infuriating as they began saying nasty things about our dear mother. *And we were not allowed to lay a finger on them.*

But we'd found their Kryptonite…their weakness. They wanted to be part of our club. We could use that to our advantage.

Dealing with an enemy is all about being one step ahead. You've got to know who they are. It's psychological. We knew who we were dealing with. Looking back, I'm a bit ashamed of myself for my involvement in the events that would follow. I know, as an adult, Carl and Jackson were little street urchins deprived of attention and in need of friends. At the time, they were lashing out and it was making things worse for them. We certainly weren't sophisticated enough to understand the socio-economic aspects of it. All we knew was that they were little a-holes who needed to learn a lesson. They would need to be taught to respect us and our property. Isn't that what all feuds are about? Our lesson plan would involve using bait and the bait was the phony offer of our own friendship.

"Do you want to join our club?"

It was an evil question for two reasons. First, we never, ever intended to give them membership to the inner circle of our friends. Also, the ingenuine offer was only being extended as a ruse to torture our pint-sized mortal enemies.

The offer was made dozens of times over the course of a few years. There was no grand plan or scheme, no end game in mind. Mostly it was used as a random retaliation after either Carl or Jackson would incense us with some heinous act of childish offense. Whenever we asked them if they wanted to join our club, there was a stipulation that went along with it. One had to prove himself worthy in order to be an esteemed member of our highly regarded and powerful gang. We knew they wanted it. No, they didn't just want it, they were begging for it. Both of these criminals would have done *anything* to be part of our nameless and non-existent club. We had to test the veracity of their desire.

Our natural born enemies were outmatched in almost every way. For instance, Jubby and I had an unspoken system of communication. It was twin telepathy. We knew what the other was thinking and feeling. When we were together our ability to be brilliantly devious was exponentially greater. Inspired by our own imaginations and dozens of action movies, we plotted our evil schemes. Most of our plans would make the boys in *The Lord of the Flies* shiver.

"If you want to join our club, you have to put this toad in your mouth for sixty seconds."

"Nooooo."

"No toad in the mouth, no club."

"Okay."

Before we knew it, a very fat and unsuspecting toad disappeared into the mouth of a boy named Jackson who had about as much intelligence as the animal that was now sitting on his tongue. Approximately five seconds went by before an impressive amount of yellow fluid started flooding out of the corners of Jackson's mouth.

"Aghhhhhhh. He's pissing in my mouth," is what I think he said. It was hard to tell because the poor little bastard had a mouthful of toad and piss. The amphibean and urine were hastily spit out.

"Sorry. Only five seconds. No club."

That's how it went from week to week. Kids can be cruel, and our hazing was varied and devious every time. At one point we spent a week peeing in a large bucket that we hung from a pulley off a branch of a maple tree. When the bucket was full, we tied a rope to its handle and dangled it to the ground. A note was written and attached to the end of the rope. It read, "If you want to join our club, stand here and pull." Flash to Jubby and me laughing uncontrollably as the urine-drenched boys scurried away from the rope they just pulled. Jackson and Carl would run home to explain to their mother why they smelled like frothy week-old piss. Their mom, Crystal, made a lot of phone calls to my parents to demand justice for our shenanigans. We were never punished. Our folks knew we were defending the neighborhood.

Our terrible pranks would almost always work. Of course, they worked. We knew who we were dealing with, and we had endlessly devious imaginations. Sometimes the pranks were even more elaborate. It really depended on the amount of retaliation we deemed necessary after they had done something awful. As all feuds do, things escalated. We had to elevate our game after Jackson had broken into our clubhouse and stolen some of our toys. Respecting our father's command and fearing a lawsuit that would result in a life of poverty, we remembered that we couldn't fight them. But we *needed* to retaliate. Screw the two wrongs don't make a right philosophy. We were in the middle of a war and a major battle was inevitable.

Armed with shovels, Jubby and I marched deep into our sacred woods. We found a perfect spot along the pathways we had created in the middle of the forest. An entire day was spent secretly digging a six-foot hole in the ground that was not unlike a grave. The hole was so big we needed a ladder to get in and out of it. Jubby was obsessed with weaponry and booby-traps at the time.

Somehow, he had found out about something called a "tiger trap." This was going to be our "tiger trap." Instead of tigers, it was going to trap scumbags.

The sun was going down and our work was almost complete. We covered the six-foot deep pit with a very stiff woolen blanket and covered the blanket with leaves, grass, and dirt. The camouflage was perfect. Nobody would ever suspect a giant hole had been dug underneath the faux forest floor we had created. The trap was set. We placed a little marker next to the concealed pit that would remind us exactly *where* our "boobys" would be trapped. The next phase of our plan was to get our targets to chase us. This wouldn't be hard. We found them in their yard grunting like cavemen and destroying some of their toys. All we had to do was yell a few derogatory names in their direction. It worked like a charm. Before you knew it, they were chasing us down the bank and through the woods. Jubby and I each jumped over our trap and turned to watch what would happen next.

It was amazing. I'd never seen anything like it. It was as if they just vanished. That's how fast they fell when their feet hit the disguised blanket and plummeted six feet into our perfectly dug trap. Holy jeez! Whooosh. Vaporized. Thud. Jubby and I looked at each other with twin-power letting us know what the other was thinking. We just killed them.

We ran over and peered down into the dark hole we had spent the entire day digging. At the bottom were the two criminals who had stolen from us. They were alive but they were stunned. They couldn't figure out what just happened. Groans and swear words were coming out of them. Justice had been served.

"That's what you get for stealing our stuff," Jubby yelled down at them.

He tapped my arm and gave me the "let's go" gesture. We walked home hearing screams and cries for help coming out of the ground. I never found out how they escaped, but when their Morticia Addams look-alike mother called our house, she wasn't pleased. It didn't matter, we won a major battle, but the war would continue.

Sometimes our enemies came in handy. We'd use them as crash test dummies for many of our inventions and experiments. One instance in which they were terribly useful was in our creation of a zip line. My mother ran a small picture framing business out of our house and had an account with the local hardware store. Bless her generous heart, she told the owner of the store that her sons could put anything from his store on her tab. That was amazing. With what seemed like immeasurable resources, we could get into all sorts of trouble. I'm sure the store owner appreciated the business, but he must have been baffled at many of the items we would put on his counter. Most likely this was true when we were purchasing pulleys, fifty yards of heavy-duty wire, wood blocks to be nailed to a tree as a ladder, giant bolts, and a two-foot square piece of wood to be used as a platform.

"What are you guys gonna build this time?" He asked.

"A zipline."

"Good luck. Don't go killing yourselves."

We knew the idea was dangerous, but it was also too good to be ignored. Nothing else in life mattered. The need to build a zipline became an obsession. Boards were nailed to a designated tree. This would create a ladder to climb to a platform installed at the top of the tree. Imagine something a trapeze artist would stand on. An old kindergarten chair was found in the attic to act as the seat on which the "zipper" would sit. Old bicycle handles were attached to the pulley to be hung on to while the zipping would take place. The line was bolted about forty feet up into the tree above the platform. It descended fifty feet to another tree below it. The line was taut. Everything was ready to go. We stood back to marvel at our ingenuity.

There was only one problem. Nobody was willing to test it out. When push came to shove, it was a great idea, but we had built a friggin' death trap. A lot of double-dog dares were issued but nobody was biting. It looked as though we may have spent a lot of time and energy building something nobody dared to use. If only we could get somebody stupid enough to test it out for us and see if it worked.

"Duh. Jackson."

"Perfect."

Our crash-test dummy was more than happy to be involved in this endeavor. Soon we were strapping dead-eyed little Jackson onto the chair with bungee cords. We feared he might bail out half-way through his descent. I remember looking up as Jubby secured the kid into position atop the platform. I wondered if we could get sued for killing a scumbag by way of lethal zipline. It was then that Jubby, without even a one-two-three-go, sent Jackson hurtling from a dangerous height on a sharp descent. You couldn't tell if the kid's scream was one of joy or terror. It must have been terror because he seemed to be trying to bail out of the seat. This proved to be impossible. Jubby had done an incredibly good job bungee cording the kids' ass in that seat good and tight. I remember being impressed with how fast he flew. I have no idea how many miles per hour it was, but it was fast. There was also a cool sound that was loud enough to be heard over Jackson's screams. It sounded exactly like a zipper being zipped for a long time…hence the name zip line.

The thing that still amazes me is that we put so much time and effort into creating our little ride, but we never put any thought into what would happen at the end of it. Jackson hit the lower tree impressively and with a loud

THUNK! The boy's screaming immediately stopped with such suddenness that it was alarming. We were all silent. We might have gone too far this time. At that moment I had an image in my head of Wile E. Coyote pancaked against a rock. The boy had stopped with an immediacy that was both alarming and hilarious. His arms and legs were both extended in front of him. He was sort of stiffly spread-eagling the tree. The impact of the blow had been absorbed mostly by his face, his torso, and his groin. We could only stare in amazement. He was not moving and remained strapped to the little kindergarten chair.

With fear that we may have just killed the kid, we peeled him from the seat. Jackson was a mess. The wind had been knocked out of him and he had blood coming out of his nose and mouth. He was gulping for air and trying to regain consciousness at the same time. When he finally found his breath, he looked up at us and asked one question.

"Now can I be in your club?"

Jubby and I looked at each other.

"Nope."

The war of Pike Street never had an official ending. No treaty or armistice was ever signed but there was one event that seemed to put a stop to things. I was eleven years old and when school started that year there was a new kid in my class. His name was Will Fox. He had the kind of red hair that would be more accurately called orange. He also had freckles all over his face. I made friends with Will and immediately liked him. It was obvious he came from the wrong side of the so-called tracks. He was more than rough around the edges and didn't take crap from anybody. I was quiet and very different from him, but we got along from the start. He wouldn't stay in school long and ended up being just a brief passer-by in my life, but he made somewhat of a profound impact in the war that had been happening on my street for years.

I was riding my bike home from school one autumn day. I had invited Will over to my house to hang out and was looking forward to getting to know my new friend. I was eager to show him the wonders of the vast wooded kingdom behind our house. As I peddled down Pike Street, I was suddenly struck in the face by an unidentified flying object.

Boom!

I flew off my bicycle and landed on the ground.

"Ahhhhhhhhh!"

I put my hand to my face. Blood was everywhere. I looked over and saw Carl next to a tree he had been hiding behind. Jackson stood next to him. They each had a rock in their hand. Those little shits had Pearl Harbored me and I had sustained a direct hit. If you've never had the pleasure of getting hit in the face by a rock and getting knocked off your bike, you should count yourself lucky. Now I found myself outnumbered and had sustained a pretty good blow. I had to retreat. They yelled some insults at me as I picked up my bike and ran it to my front yard.

An hour later Will showed up at my door.

"What the hell happened to your face?"

Will Fox was looking at the black eye that had been the result of being ambushed by my neighbors. I had previously told him about Carl and Jackson, so he already knew about the Pike Street feud that had been going on for years. When I explained how I had sustained my new shiner, he listened with a menacing grin on his heavily freckled face. He nodded intently and seemed to be formulating a plan for retaliation. When I was finished, he waited a few seconds before he asked a chilling question with terrible implications.

"Got any gasoline?"

What the hell did that mean?

"Yeah. Out in the garage," I said.

"Good. Follow me."

My heart started racing. Was he serious? Gasoline? What was he going to do? I couldn't show weakness. He was a new friend. I had to be tough and go along with whatever devious plan had entered his mind. My reputation depended on it. The one thing an eleven-year-old boy doesn't want to be thought of is a sissy.

We went to the garage. Right next to the lawnmower was a half-filled, red gasoline can.

"There it is."

Will grabbed it and headed toward the Winger house. I followed. What the hell was he going to do? I started to get nervous. Maybe my new friend is a god-damned arsonist? This wasn't going to be good. He stopped in front of their house with the gas can hanging from his freckly little fist. Squinting over the property he set his sights on the sandbox in the back corner of the yard. Before I knew it, Will was pouring gasoline over the sandbox where Carl and Jackson's precious Tonka-Trucks were scattered all over. These were sacred to them.

I watched in awe, frozen in place. Was this really happening? When Will was satisfied with the amount of gasoline he had used he turned to me.

"Go up and knock on the door. Then run back here and stand next to me."

"Okay," I said, feeling nervous and uneasy.

I knocked and quickly ran back to take my place next to my psychotic new friend's side. He might be a sociopath, but he was my sociopath.

The two witless instigators who had recently ambushed me came out to the porch.

"Did you hit my friend with a rock?"

"Yeah."

"Never again."

Suddenly Will pulled a god-damned Zippo lighter out of his back pocket. A god-damned Zippo lighter! What kind of kid has a Zippo lighter? One click and it was ignited. As a "holy crap" look was plastered on my face, Will threw his Zippo on top of the sandbox that he had just flooded with gasoline. Whoooosh! Instant Tonka Truck bonfire. I felt an incredible amount of white-hot heat blast across my face as my bowl haircut blew away from my eleven-year-old forehead.

The screams of my two little nemeses were ear piercing.

"OUR TRUCKS! NOOOOO!"

Will tapped me to turn around and walk back to my house. We walked away like the action heroes in movies…in slow motion with an explosion raging in the background…bad ass look on Will's face and a horrified expression on mine. It was great having a new friend, although I feared our relationship might lead me down a path toward a life of crime.

After good old Crystal called my parents about this doozy, my father expressed concern that we'd be sued. Luckily, that would never happen. Scumbags are mostly full of bark and very little bite. What did happen was that the war on Pike Street thoroughly came to an end.

7

Altar Boys Going to Hell

Memories of church bring back a myriad of feelings. As an adult, thinking about going to church when I was a kid, I remember a constant feeling that I would be going to Hell. Due to many factors, I still feel like a fiery pit might be my final destination.

I believe in God, or a Superior Power, or whatever people want to call it. I'm comfortable accepting my inability to understand it all but I certainly spend a lot of time wondering about it. My Catholic childhood provided a foundation for my curiosity. The experiences I had growing up in the Catholic Church gave me not only a sense of reverence, but also an appreciation for the absurd. The world is wonderfully ridiculous above all other things. There is comedy everywhere, and a sense of humor might be the best defense against almost anything. Nothing ever made as much sense to me as *Monty Python*. Life is just wacky and not to be taken too seriously. "If you don't laugh, you have to cry," is an axiom that springs to mind. Not much is sacred and almost everything is kind of funny…especially church. Going to church helped establish my sense of humor and allowed me to find spiritual, mental, and emotional salvation through an appreciation of laughter.

When Jubby and I got to the ripe old age of eight, my father insisted that we become altar boys. He thought that our, and more importantly his, salvation would improve significantly if we were to serve the Lord on the altar every Sunday. I had misgivings and feared this was a bad idea but, like a good Catholic boy, I just did what I was told.

The Church was a mystical but scary place to me. The Stations of the Cross surrounding the entire congregation were enough to give nightmares to any kid for the rest of his life. It was worse for a sensitive kid with a strong imagination and an inclination to worry. I had a hard time focusing on the sermons. I was too transfixed by all the gore surrounding me. Adults are desensitized to it, but to a kid the scenery in the Catholic church can be a horror show. Old St. Pat's Church didn't shy away from it. Statues telling the story of the Crucifixion lined every wall. The Passion, in all its tortured detail, was everywhere you looked. From the time I could sit up, I remember looking around the room trying to figure out what was going on. What was all the torture and suffering all about?

The real capper in the church was a life-size statue of Jesus prominently hanging on the cross at the front of the altar. It was prominent. You walk in the front door and boom, Jesus Christ! He didn't look like a statue. Everything about him seemed realistic. Did I mention he was life-sized? The sculptor had gone the whole nine yards and chosen to make all the gore as believable as possible. There were holes in all the right places, bleeding gashes, a wicked crown of thorns, and a particular anguish written on the face of the Savior.

Jesus Christ!

Literally!

And there I sat Sunday after Sunday looking up at it, trying to comprehend the meaning of it all. It isn't Disneyland inside a Catholic church, not by a long shot.

My twin brother and I had gone through the entire spiel: Baptism, First Confession, and First Communion. We memorized the Lord's Prayer, The Hail Mary, and the Act of Contrition. We went to every weekly religious education class, every Sunday mass, and every Holy Day of Obligation. It all seemed terrifyingly important and we were expected to sit down, shut up, and listen. Asking questions wasn't really a thing we did. Inquisitiveness wasn't encouraged in this world. If we did ask questions, the answers were not terribly helpful. One exchange between myself and one of the nicer nuns said it all. I was curious about Holy Communion.

"So, we're actually eating Jesus?" I asked.

"Yes."

"We're actually eating his body?" I pressed.

"It's called transubstantiation. It's the belief that the wafer becomes the actual body of Christ during the mass."

Long pause…

"Isn't that cannibalism?"

"God hears everything. Do you want to go to Hell?"

I shut up.

It was like that a lot. I just learned to stay quiet. Sometimes it's better not to ask questions. However, an internal conversation started in my mind and has never really stopped. Religion is fascinating to me. Talking to people about their beliefs and their experiences from childhood can be awesome, especially finding commonalities and exploring the nature of belief and faith from different viewpoints. Growing up as a Catholic created curiosity in me and inspired a fascination with the thinking of others and the mystery of a higher power.

Most likely my lifelong fascination was inspired, in part, by my years serving on the altar. One fateful day I found myself marching up to the church with Jubby. We were given orders to meet with the priest to be trained to be altar boys. Before I knew it, I was wearing the classic robes of the priest's little sidekick. I quickly learned the ins and outs of the job. It wasn't that difficult. Light some candles while looking solemn. Ring some bells while looking solemn. Deliver the bread and wine to the priest while looking solemn. Hold a cross here. Hold a candle there. Make the sign of the cross at the appropriate time. Stand. Sit. Kneel. Stand. Sit. Kneel. Chant, a lot. Try to block out the singing of the tone-deaf organist who managed to sound like a cat whose tail was caught in a garbage disposal. Then there was the most important job of all. Do not ever laugh when one of your fellow altar boys farts in the middle of a service. That was pretty much it. Repeatedly. Sunday after bloody Sunday.

The worst thing about church when you're a kid is that it's boring. There's such a lack of anything different that it is truly mind-numbing. The strict expectation was for you to have to wake up early on your Sunday off from school, go to a place filled with scary iconography, shut up and just sit there. Open rebellion against this was not an option. What would you expect a kid, his twin brother, and his best friends to do other than make every attempt to entertain themselves against the threat of boredom at an existential level? Simply put, there's a good chance I will be going to Hell, if it exists, because the Catholic Church failed to entertain me when I was a kid. What were we supposed to do? We were forced to entertain ourselves or be bored to death. We didn't have a choice.

One of the things I dreaded most in church was saying Rosaries. I think everybody did. When the priest announced a surprise Rosary, you could feel a collective sigh from the congregation.

"Folks, today we will be saying a Rosary."

"Uhhhhhhhh."

A Rosary, to a kid, is a test of will power. Saying one was like running a marathon. It felt like it was going to last forever. Somehow a twenty-minute prayer had a magical way of making time slow to a complete halt. Slow and agonizing repeated chanting in which you mindlessly drone out the same words baffled me and tested my undiagnosed attention deficit disorder. It seemed like saying a thousand prayers in a row wasn't communicating with God so much as it was a test of patience and endurance.

Rosaries became a hell of a lot more fun to say in church when my friend James, a fellow altar boy, developed a condition in which he would faint half-way through the process. It was awesome! We'd all be kneeling, saying prayer after prayer just looking over waiting for the moment to watch him go down. Right in the middle of the "Hail Mary" – Timber!! Thunk! There was James, in full altar boy get-up, twitching around with his eyeballs rolled back in his head. Jesus was on the cross looking down at a kid appearing to be having a seizure. The priest wouldn't miss a beat. Like a praying machine, he would continue the Rosary and nod for us to pick our friend up, take him to the room at the back of the church and get him together. We would imagine we were like soldiers taking a fallen comrade off the battlefield to get medical attention. Finally, we had a little excitement during mass.

As we got older and our boredom with church's repetitiveness got worse, we were forced to entertain ourselves by doing the usual things: Make faces when you thought nobody was looking, flipping each other off when you thought nobody was looking, stealing a sip of wine when you thought nobody was looking, and letting out a fart in a well-timed attempt to get your fellow altar boys to be sent into spasms of laughter. There's nothing worse than being in church and trying not to laugh. Attempting to stifle the giggles when it's inappropriate, especially after somebody squeaks out the dreaded flatulence, only leads to some kind of temporary insanity in which the person laughing uncontrollably has forgotten why they were laughing in the first place and is only aware of two things: Wondering if it's possible to die of uncontrollable laughter and absolute certainty that the non-amused people staring at you are going to call the authorities to throw you in the looney bin. It's a terrible situation for sure.

I'm pretty sure the years that my friends and I were altar boys served as banner years for attendance in St. Patrick's Church. I don't think it had anything to do with a spike in religious faith but, rather, because they were entertained by four idiots completely unaware that all their on-altar grab-ass could be seen by everyone. It's funny to think back and realize that we, as most kids do, thought we were getting away with things. People, I'm sure, just found us to be amusing idiots and didn't care enough to do anything about it. We were the Marx Brothers dressed up as altar boys. Their assessment was accurate. We were morons.

One time, Jubby had no problem asking our religious education teacher, Sister Rosemary, if she'd ever seen the movie *Rosemary's Baby*. What a dumb question to ask a nun. It's even dumber when one considers that the very title of the movie implies that the main character, named Rosemary, has had a baby. Every kid should know that any conversation with a nun that even hints at the idea of sex is a terrible idea. Sister Rosemary just looked confused. To be fair. So did we. Sometimes kids don't know when to keep their mouths shut.

Another time, my career as an altar boy almost led me towards priesthood. The horror! Our parish was scheduled to host a Holy Day of Obligation service. Priests and nuns came from all over the area. Apparently, it was a big deal. Our priest was worried his gang of unpredictable altar boys might pull their usual shenanigans and embarrass him in front of all his peers. Father Francis was a kind and generous man and we never wanted to disappoint him. Somehow, we were able to get through this special mass without acting like the Four Stooges.

It was a miracle. We served the entire ceremony and nobody farted or did anything stupid. I tried particularly hard to appear as solemn as a ten-year-old boy could. I just concentrated on looking sad while doing all the jobs required of me during the mass. This was not difficult because looking somber came easily to me. Even though I was a relatively happy kid, I just happened to have a naturally forlorn appearance. I was rail-thin and gave the impression that I was not fed at home. I probably weighed about eighty pounds soaking wet and was whiter than a piece of rice in a snowstorm. My bowl haircut didn't help. I didn't smile much due to the fact I was self-conscious about the giant gap in my front teeth. Furthermore, I was quiet and sensitive. A quiet kid is often mistaken for a sad kid. I wasn't sad, I just looked that way.

I mention how I looked because, apparently, it was the reason one of the visiting priests decided to come to the back room after the mass was over. The man wanted to have a serious discussion with me. Nobody else. Just me. I was back in my street clothes. Patrick, James Jubby, and I were getting ready to leave the Church when the priest stopped us. He was on a mission from God. The man was truly frightening. He reminded me of Skeletor from He-Man.

"Stop right there, boys."

We froze. Oh, crap. What did we do now? Nobody farted. Nobody flipped another person off. Nobody laughed inappropriately. What could it be?

"I want to talk with you."

He pointed his bony finger right at me. Uh-oh.

"My son, you have a look about you. The light of God shines from you."

What the hell is he smoking?

"Uhhhhh."

"God is calling you, my son."

"Huh?"

"God is calling you to become a priest, my son."

I was terrified. This man was determining my future. You can't argue with a priest or you'll go to Hell.

"But…I like girls."

"That's no matter, my son. Let me ask you a question. Do you know who Jonah was?"

"No."

Catholic kids don't know anything when it comes to the Bible…especially Old Testament stuff.

The priest continued, "Jonah was swallowed by a whale. Do you know why?"

"No."

Where was he going with this?

"Jonah had been called by God, just like you're being called. Jonah tried to ignore the call and was swallowed by a whale to teach him a lesson. Do you know what the lesson was?"

Silence.

"Jonah couldn't ignore God's call. Neither can you."

"But I don't want to be a priest."

"Don't ignore the call, my son. Don't be swallowed by a whale."

Then he left.

Are you kidding me? What the hell was I supposed to do with that? That's some seriously heavy nonsense to lay on a little kid. My friends and brother thought it was hilarious. They started calling me "Father Brendan" all the time. It might have been funny to them, but it scared the crap out of me. As far as I knew priests were the major authority in the world. This Skeletor-looking priest had done a number on me. In desperation I went to my parents to explain my concern. I told them I didn't want to be a priest. To my super-duper Captain Catholic father, having a son who became a priest would have been a huge gain for his ever-lasting salvation. However, instead of pushing the idea on me, he must have noticed my deep anxiety and told me I hadn't been called. I could go on liking girls, and I didn't have to be a priest if I didn't want to be a priest. It would take some time but eventually I let myself off the hook.

Most likely, I'm still going to Hell though and probably so are my fellow altar boy buddies. The non-Catholic kids in school were jealous of my posse of altar boys. Patrick, James, Jubby and I stood apart because of our denomination. We were the only Catholic kids in school. Our secular peers figured we were part of a cult, but they were also jealous because the four of us were regularly allowed to get out of school. The greatest thing about being an altar boy was serving funerals. Whenever a Catholic person in town would die my friends would celebrate. We weren't happy for somebody dying. We were just psyched to get out of school for a day.

Every kid in school must have assumed that a Catholic funeral was a ridiculously long affair. The four of us would usually leave early in the morning and serve the mass for an hour. After the funeral was over, we had to think of ways to extend our break. We would usually sneak down to someone's house and play Nintendo for a few hours as school was still going on. Eventually we'd make it back for the very end of the day. If people pressed us about why we were gone so long, we'd usually be able to come up with a good reason right on the spot.

"We had to clean the church."

You know, tell a lie. We figured we could confess our sins to the priest later.

Other than getting out of school, the best part of having to serve funerals was that we got paid. It wasn't a lot, but we would each score a few bucks from the family of the deceased in the form of a tip. The money always burned a hole in our pockets pretty fast. We'd race to the small grocery store on Main Street and buy as much candy as we could.

Throughout the years we served dozens of funerals. Some were very sad. Some were big. Some were depressingly small. During all of them we tried our best not to act like little yahoos. Most of the time, we were able to pull it off. However, one funeral would prove to be our undoing, and it's the reason God might be slamming Heaven's door on me and my fellow altar boys.

An old lady had passed away. She was the matriarch of a large family in town and had died of old age. We were given the call to leave school and serve the funeral. All the pews were full. Like I said, it was a large family. The mourners were typically sad. Mind you, it was one of those funerals where nobody was in shock or surprised. The lady was ancient, and people would miss her, but it wasn't necessarily a tragedy. The immediate family was at the head of the church. She had a few sons who were grown men, and they all had their families surrounding them in the pews. The church was packed full of solemn-faced mourners paying their respects. We were doing a great job. There had been no mockery or goofing around. Nothing had gone wrong. It seemed like this was going to be a solid effort on our part…until the final portion of the ceremony.

Before a funeral mass, the altar boy duties had to be divided up. I was easy-going and never gave a damn what job I was going to have; neither did Patrick or James for that matter. Jubby, being somewhat of a pyromaniac, always wanted any job that involved lighting a fire. Lighting candles was okay but there was one job during a funeral that was the best of all. That was lighting the charcoal to burn the incense. Jubby always got that job.

Towards the end of the funeral, the priest and altar boys gathered around the closed casket for a final prayer. The coffin sat in the middle aisle next to the family and in front of the altar where the statue of Jesus was hanging on the cross looking over the events.

At this point in the ceremony every one of us knew that it was important to keep ourselves together. There are quite a few moving parts at the end of the mass before they wheel the dead person out to be planted in the ground. Three altar boys stand at the foot of the coffin. The boy in the middle holds a six-foot iron pole with a cross at the top. He is flanked by two other altar boys holding three-foot-tall lit candles. They are to stand at the foot of the coffin, hold their instruments, and look solemn. Easy enough. On this occasion, I held the cross while Patrick and James were my candle-bearing wingmen. Jubby had the all-important job of being responsible for what we called "The Clanker."

I have no idea what it was actually called but it looked like a golden football. It had a base at one end and a chain on the other. It had holes all over its sides. The metal device weighed about five pounds and could be pulled apart to place a piece of charcoal within it. The altar boy, in this case my twin brother, would light the charcoal and then place holy incense on top of the embers that had just been lit. The canister would be closed and locked in. We called it "The Clanker" because the priest would swing it in mid-air with the intention of banging the heavy part of it against the chain to make a "clanking" sound. All the while it would be sending weird-smelling smoke from the burning incense through the holes and into the air. Catholic symbolism was always right in front of you. You imagined the smoke rising from The Clanker mimicking the soul of the deceased rising to Heaven.

There was more to Jubby's duty than just lighting up The Clanker, though. He was also supposed to be the priest's little "wingman." He had to remain at the priest's elbow and follow him around holding all the necessary devices the priest needed to use. These devices would be listed as The Clanker, the Funeral Service Booklet, and a bucket of holy water.

Picture this. A congregation of mourners filled the church. I'm holding a cross at the end of the coffin. My two friends, holding candles, are beside me. The priest is at the front of the coffin conducting the service and my ten-year old twin brother is right next to him. Latin prayers are chanted. The priest then asks my brother for the bucket of holy water. This is promptly handed to him. Then the holy man circles around the coffin with dead old lady resting inside and proceeds to sprinkle it with holy water from the wand he dips into the bucket. He does all whilst chanting Latin prayers. Phase one is complete.

Now for phase two. The priest asks my brother for The Clanker that has a burning piece of charcoal inside recently lit by Jubby just minutes before. He slowly circles the coffin chanting and clanking away. After he is done lapping the coffin, he hands the so-called "Clanker" back to my brother standing at the foot of the altar. That is when all holy hell breaks loose. You see, Jubby had not properly secured the device. The Clanker was not tightly screwed in place. When the priest handed it back to him the entire thing came apart in his hands. It divided into two parts and fell to the floor. Crash!! The burning charcoal spilled out and was rolling all over the altar. Burning incense was scattered everywhere.

Jubby, in a state of panic, totally forgot where he was. As a couple hundred funeral goers stood with mouths agape, my brother in full altar boy costume, ran to a burning piece of charcoal on the ground and picked it up with his bare hand.

"SHIIIIIIITT!!"

That's what he yelled in the middle of the church in front of all those mourners. In a state of panic, he had forgotten that picking up burning charcoal would burn the hell out of his ten-year-old little hand. He also forgot his place and yelled an obscenity in the shadow of Jesus hanging on the cross. To top it all off my brother, having burned his hand on the charcoal, needed relief from his third-degree wound. Still forgetting where he was, he quickly stuck his hand in the bucket of holy water conveniently sitting on the altar.

I watched in total disbelief. I'd seen my brother pull some doozies over the years, but this was ridiculous. You could feel the entire congregation's shock at what just happened. The Holy Savior never looked so ashamed. When Jesus was crucified, he asked God, "Father, forgive them for they know not what they do." I had that same thought regarding my brother at this absurd moment in time. God, forgive him. He does not know what he is doing.

I'm not sure how we were able to get through the rest of the mass, but we did. We were all in shock. My brother had accidentally dumped burning charcoal on an altar during a funeral mass, tried to pick it up with his bare hands, yelled an obscenity in church in front of an entire congregation, and then extinguished his burning hand inside a bucket of holy water. Jesus, Mary, and Joseph!

The four of us found ourselves in the back room of the church. None of us were talking. We just knew we were going to be in deep, deep trouble. Do altar boys get fired? We certainly felt we deserved it at this point.

The son of the woman who died came into the back room. He was a tall man dressed in a black suit. He looked pissed. His eyes looked all of us over until they stopped on Jubby. I could feel my brother squirming.

"You!" the man said as he pointed at Jubby.

"I'm sorry," my brother said.

"Don't be."

"What?"

"That was the funniest god-damned thing I've ever seen. Here. You guys split this up."

He pulled a hundred-dollar bill out of his wallet and gave it to my brother. "Don't spend it all in one place."

We ran to the store as fast as we could. We spent every single cent on candy then went to a back alley in town and gorged ourselves until we were sick. All those scary nuns used to tell us that gluttony was one of the Seven Deadly Sins. We didn't care. We figured we were probably going to Hell anyway.

8

Cub Scouts vs. Nazis

I was ten years old when I got into my first brawl. It was at Cub Scout camp, and it happened to be against a bunch of god-damned Nazis.

One of the essential lessons of growing up is discovering the difference between the good guys and the bad guys. Hopefully you can learn right and wrong, but it's just as essential to be able to decipher between douche bags and non-douche bags. There is an invisible marker in time in everyone's childhood when they discover that the world has a lot of a-holes in it. Once one realizes this disappointing fact, there is no turning back. You've come a little bit closer to the adult world where you will always be trying to keep the awful people away from you and the good people close to you.

I was lucky when I was a kid because I had great friends. Your friends help you realize what you stand for and who your enemies are going to be. We were a little gang of rugrats. There was nothing special about us other than the fact that we were tight with each other. Our loyalty was unspoken, but it was deeply felt. We all had our signature trait. I was quiet, Jubby was wild, Patrick liked to hunt, James was athletic, Josh was squirrely, Raymond liked Batman, and Fred was the one we all picked on. There must be a Fred in every group. We didn't have much, but we had each other.

It never really dawned on us that our families didn't have all that much money. None of us were destitute, just middle-class kids and not one of us was spoiled. We had our bikes, the streets, the back woods, and our imaginations. It was all we needed.

Being part of a gang can be a vital part of growing up. At its best a gang is a family of friends who share similar values. Those values reinforce your sense of identity and self-worth. To be part of a gang is to know that you belong and that you matter to others. We didn't stand for anything except each other.

Ten-year-old boys spend a lot of time doing a lot of stupid things. They spend a lot of time teasing each other and "busting each other's balls." From the outside looking in, it can appear obnoxious and cruel at times. But it's not. What most people don't see is the invisible bond that exists. Nobody signs a form or anything. Blood brother pacts don't have to be made. There's just an unspoken idea that exists throughout the gang. You don't know exactly why, but for some reason you'll do anything to stick up for your group. It's true loyalty.

I came to understand the value of friendship during the summer before I went into fifth grade. One of us had seen a flyer in the Post Office advertising the opportunity to become a Cub Scout. We all looked over the flyer and immediately knew we wanted to do it. The pictures of Cub Scout life were seductive. Every part of the pamphlet was amazing. Kids our age were shown white water rafting, camping outdoors, and hiking in the woods. They all had these huge shit-eating grins on their little shit-eating Cub Scout faces. Advertising works on ten-year-olds and we were sold immediately. The thing that really grabbed us the most was the uniforms. All the kids in the flyer were wearing these super sharp, blue shirts and had yellow neckerchiefs on. They had badges everywhere. To me they looked like miniature elite soldiers. We were transfixed by the propaganda. I wanted to look exactly like the kids in the pictures. We all did.

A plan was formulated. We had to ask our parents if we could join the Cub Scouts. The eight of us organized our talking points and went directly to work convincing our folks that it was imperative to our futures to become Cub Scouts. It turned out to be easy to convince them. We showed them the pamphlet.

"Can we be Cub Scouts, please?"

"Does it cost anything?"

"No."

"Just try not to kill yourselves."

That was it. We all got the thumbs up. The next step was to meet our Cub Scout Master. Meeting him would teach me the difference between how I thought things *would* be and how they *would actually* be. The chasm of difference between what you expect something to be like and what it ends up really being like can be enormous. Growing up is all about learning to deal with disappointment. Eventually you get used to the idea that things aren't going to go the way you originally thought they would. Often, it's not the kid's fault. They don't stand a chance, surrounded by an adult world intent on selling a lot of malarkey. The pamphlet that inspired us turned out to be pure unadulterated, grade "A" bullshit. We would find that out the day of our first Cub Scout meeting.

Our Scout Master was a Korean War veteran named Stan. He spent most of his days drinking cheap beer on the little front steps of the trailer he lived in. This death-trap of a home also happened to be the site of our meetings. We walked up to his trailer with some trepidation. Picture a man in his mid-fifties with a cigarette in one hand and a beer in the other. He was sitting on his porch, wearing sunglasses and a red Budweiser trucker hat he probably nabbed at some flea market. The only kind of shirt he wore was a V-neck T-shirt with all sorts of weird stains down the front of it. Jeans and Velcro-strapped tennis shoes completed the look. He smelled of stale beer and unfiltered cigs. Upon first meeting, he didn't seem too kid friendly. It wasn't an illusion; the man didn't give a flying fart about kids. He seemed like the kind of person who never actually even existed as a kid. The day he was born, he probably walked straight out of his mother's birth canal as an old man smoking a cigarette, drinking a beer and bitching about how immigrants and minorities were taking over the world. I imagine his employment as a Cub Scout Master was due to some kind of forced community service for public urination or something. Hell, for all I know the guy was a pedophile. Back then parents didn't really vet people too much. For some reason, they thought child molesters only drove around in white vans and offered candy. Either way, my parents didn't ask too many questions about the guy.

Not to be put off from what we were imagining, we gave Stan the pamphlet and excitedly asked him when we were going to get to do the things it was advertising. He looked it over through his aviators with a Marlboro hanging from his mouth. We waited eagerly to see what his response would be.

"Yeah…We're not gonna be doing much of that shit."

"No white water rafting?"

"See any boats in my yard, kid?"

"Nope."

"No hiking?"

"Probably not."

"Uniforms?"

"Doubt it."

"So, what are we gonna do?"

"You guys want to learn how to start a fire?"

"Sure."

We had to start somewhere. It didn't involve rubbing sticks together or doing it in any "Cub Scout" type way. He just splashed a little lighter fluid on some logs and lit a match. The flyer would be thrown in the trash. We would spend one week a night going to Stan's house to have our meetings and learn how to do "Cub Scout things." "Cub Scout things" mostly meant hanging out with Stan, watching him drink beer, smoke cigarettes and tell us age-inappropriate stories about prostitutes and war. Probably the most profound session was the one when we ended up learning a ton of new swear words while Stan tried to remember how to tie a sailor's knot. At least our vocabularies were improving. Another session was spent telling the bunch of us why we could never trust a woman. You know, Cub Scout stuff.

Somewhere along the way Stan got a pamphlet that was advertising Cub Scout camp at a place called Camp Elk Lick located deep in the back woods of Pennsylvania. Oh great, another pamphlet to seduce us only to have our dreams crushed by reality. It didn't matter; we got super-excited again. Attending camp felt like our lives depended on it and the world would end if we didn't. A sales pitch was made to the parents. We must have done a good job because they all agreed to let us go. Before long, we were being dropped off at Camp Elk Lick with hundreds of other ten-year-old Cub Scouts.

The place was gorgeous, straight out of a post card picture. A vast wooded area was surrounded by an enormous glistening pond. As soon as you pulled into the parking lot you could see a large council house with a giant covered porch. It looked over a vast lawn that descended about fifty yards only to be interrupted by the most pristine body of water I'd ever seen. The pond was perfect. Canoes and paddle boats lined the water's edge. What could be better than spending a week during the hot summer splashing around in such a magnificent pond!

There were cabins scattered here and there and paths that led to various campsites throughout the woods and independent of one another. Word had it that every campsite was different from the other. They each had their own name and characteristics. Most were named after Native American Indian tribes…not exactly politically correct by future standards. But there was one campsite that was legendary. It was called *Mount Rushmore*. The name hinted at its majesty. It was supposedly the best campsite, and every camper knew about it before coming to camp. Mount Rushmore was aptly named. It overlooked the entire location and was scattered with boulders the size of houses. It had been prominently featured throughout the brochure. What were the chances we could get Mount Rushmore? We doubted it would happen but crossed our fingers and hoped for the best. Whatever troop got to set tents up underneath this site's magnificent boulders were the luckiest kids at the camp.

Our parents stuck around for a few seconds to meet the camp staff before taking off. The counselors seemed nice, that is, until our parents said good-bye. Initial appearances were deceiving. Once all the parents were gone, a transformation took place. It was swift and unexpected. The minute my folk's Oldsmobile was out of sight the counselors, who had previously been glad-handing our parents, changed. I had watched them greeting all the moms and dads with big toothy grins, assuring them that their sons were in good hands. Now that all the parents were gone, the counselors turned on us with menacing looks on their faces.

"All right, you little turds. Mommy and daddy are gone so let's get one thing straight. You're not gonna give us any crap. What we say goes. There are rules here."

Oh, man. That was a tonal shift we were not expecting. This wasn't a joke. This was how it was going to be all week. For the next hour they berated us and established their dominance with arbitrary threats. At only eighteen years old, the young counselors had power for the first time in their lives and they were not above abusing it. Things really got serious when they made their final point. It was obviously all for show, but they went on and on about how there was one sure-fired way to find ourselves going home immediately.

"Do you see that pond out there? Do you? If one of you little turds steps foot inside that pond without our say so, mommy and daddy are getting called and we're going to be waving bye-bye to your little asses. Got it?"

When you're a kid, you get used to seeing people on power-trips. Your life is a constant reminder of just how much power you *don't* have. The only way to navigate it is through ridicule. That's the contract. If you want to wield power over others, you're going to be the butt of a few jokes. My group of friends knew how to shut up in front of authority, but we were also geniuses when it came to one thing, we knew how to mock people when they weren't looking. When their backs were turned or when they weren't around, we delighted in cutting our targets to pieces with impressions, jokes, and taunts. It's an under-appreciated survival skill of a kid. You must follow a lot of rules and you don't get to make a lot of your own choices. You don't have to like it but you sure can mock it. Making fun of the rules and the rule-makers gets you through.

This pond rule was apparently a big deal. They weren't messing around. I guess some kid drowned a long time ago and they'd been told to be real hard asses when it came to enforcing the law of not swimming without supervision. It didn't matter. We got it. Don't go in the pond unless the counselors say so. It didn't seem like a rule that would be too hard to follow.

Needless to say, the Jekyll and Hyde transformation with the counselors freaked us out. Suddenly we had the feeling that Camp Elk Lick might not be all that the brochure cracked it up to be and it wasn't long before we realized there was something else terribly wrong. There were hundreds of boys going to this camp from dozens of Cub Scout troops. Something was immediately obvious; we were *different* from all the other troops. Not in a good way. We stood out like turds in a punch bowl. We didn't look like the other groups. It was obvious. And there was no way to hide it.

"Look at the *poor* kids," was the taunt.

Every other group had uniforms. They had matching hats, matching shirts, matching sashes, and badges galore. They all saluted and sang songs in unison while marching. They all brought fancy camping gear and tents. It was apparent that every other Cub Scout troop came from money, and it showed. We were a small group of rag-tag kids wearing T-shirts, ripped jeans, and scuffed up sneakers. We couldn't march, couldn't sing songs, and couldn't tie knots, but if you gave us some lighter fluid, we might be able to start a fire. We knew how to swear but that might not help the current situation. We stood out immediately and there was no way to hide it.

"Look at what they're wearing. Look at the poor kids."

The collective group taunt had begun. Cruelty in a mob of little kids can spread like contagion. Once it starts, there's no real cure. We had no defense against what was about to happen.

"Look at the poor kids…they don't even have uniforms…they're wellys… welfare kids, welfare kids, welfare kids."

Jeez. What the hell did we get ourselves into? The counselors were a-holes and so were all the other campers. This reality hit us immediately and we were crushed. Our hopes of having a good time were destroyed. Now we felt sick, and the spotlight was on us. There was no escaping it. Once cruelty begins it's hard to stop, maybe impossible. Sometimes kids are no different from adults, both follow the age-old script written by human history.

There was one Cub Scout troop that was head and shoulders meaner than the others. These kids were Nazis. I'm serious. They had their Cub Scout shit together. Not only did they have the nicest uniforms and ass-loads of patches, but they took marching and singing and all that stuff to a whole other level. It was like they were born with merit badges on their diapers for taking the best dumps or something. They were fantastically cruel as well. They were the first ones to call us out on being "poor" and "wellys" and getting everyone else turned against our group.

We had never felt anything like this. Home was a long way away. Nobody was there to help and we felt sick with sadness. We wanted to be here so badly and now all our hopes of having fun had been dashed into smithereens. How would we survive the week? We knew one thing, we'd have to rely on each other.

Mobs and gangs are different things, but they can share a few similarities. They are almost always some kind of cult of personality. There is usually somebody in charge that establishes the attitude of the group. The Cub Scout Nazis were no different. They had a definite leader. His name wasn't Adolf, but he was like a ten-year-old Hitler wet dream. Tall. Athletic build. Ice blue eyes that radiated hatred toward everything they looked at. His blond hair was slicked back with some kind of hair product that made it look hard and plastic. He had an angry mouth; always turned down at the corners. The expression he had on his face was as though he had just taken a bite of turd sandwich. The sound of his voice dripped with pure contempt. Everybody in his group was his minion. A Nazi youth was alive and well in 1984. Later in my life I would read the *Harry Potter* books and be introduced to the character of Draco Malfoy. This kid was a living, breathing Draco Malfoy in the flesh and he had set his sights on us, the so-called poor kids. The sight of our T-shirts and blue jeans made him want to puke out of elitist disdain.

Eventually, the orientation meeting took place in the Council House. The counselors had us all sitting at long tables in the large banquet room. My group huddled in a corner keeping our distance. Camp was being kicked off with all sorts of speeches and directions. Above everything campers were eager to find out one thing: *What camp site they would get?* Everyone wanted Mount Rushmore, the camp site with the giant boulders. Site after site was announced and given to one troop after another. Each troop would groan with disappointment after hearing their site wasn't going to be Mount Rushmore. Throughout the Council House fingers were crossed for the lucky draw. Prayers were silently said.

"Please, please, God, let it be us."

Our troop was announced next to last. The other troop whose site hadn't been announced just so happened to be the troop of Nazis who had swiftly established themselves as the superior troop of the camp. When they called our troops' name, the other boys yelled all sorts of nasty things about us being scummy and all kinds of other mean crap. It hurt. We just sat in a kind of shame until everyone was told to quiet down. Once there was silence, the counselor making the announcement commenced and said the name of *our* troop again and then the words we were hoping for, "Mount Rushmore." Holy shit! *We* won the cool camp site. We were going to be able to camp under the boulders. The Nazis didn't get the site. We got it. It was unbelievable.

Unfortunately, we also got something else along with Mount Rushmore. Every camper at the camp hated us before because we looked poor and were different from them. Now they *really* hated us because we got the best campsite. Be careful what you wish for and all that stuff.

We left the Council House eager to get away from the derision and the insults being thrown at us from hundreds of jealous and spiteful Cub Scouts. You can imagine the comments, "They only gave the poor kids Mount Rushmore because they felt sorry for them." We hiked through the woods and eventually arrived at our site. It was immediately apparent why everyone was jealous. I'd never seen anything like it. The boulders were enormous. Each was as big as a house. You could climb to the top and feel like a god. It would have been a dangerous twenty-foot drop if one were to fall off. At the bottom of the rocks were gnarly briars and thorn bushes you wouldn't want to fall in anyway. We set up our tents and tucked in for the night. It had been a long day. We didn't know what discrimination was. We just felt bad from the events of the day. Suddenly, we were thought of as "the poor kids" and knew one thing: When the sun came up and we had to interact with the other campers, we were going to have to face more insults.

We woke up to rain in the morning. It was pouring out and the plans for outdoor activities had to be changed. Most troops just stayed at their sites waiting out the downpour. We decided to go to the Council House. Unfortunately, the only other group that was there just so happened to be Draco Malfoy and his band of Hitler Youth. We were told to eat breakfast and then go out to the covered porch to entertain ourselves. Counselors were always trying to get rid of us. It's quite possible they were more interested in going off in the woods and smoking dope while we remained unsupervised.

The rain continued while we sat on the porch of the Council House overlooking the long green yard leading down to the pond, forbidden to us. We sat, bored, listening to the rain pelting down on the roof. Then the Nazis marched out to join us. Crap. They were led by their blonde leader, Draco. Ughhh. The commentary from the other day picked up almost immediately, mostly unoriginal references to us being on welfare. We didn't know how to respond. Coming from this group, the derision stung most. You couldn't ignore their attitude of superiority.

Eventually the dialogue shifted into a competitive game of Simon Says, at least it started out as Simon Says. The game quickly turned into a game of dare. While the rain continued to come down, we faced off against the Nazis daring each other with thinly disguised tests of manliness. It started out small.

"Simon says lick the table."

But it escalated quickly.

"Simon says…eat some grass."

"Simon says…pick your nose and eat a booger."

"Simon says…moon the counselors."

Then it got out of hand. Draco had sized us up. He had a keen sense to pick out the leader of our group. We didn't really have a leader, we had Jubby. He stood out as the most aggressive of us and he looked like a kid who didn't take shit from anyone. Draco picked up on this and wanted to puff his chest out against my twin brother. It was clearly alpha-male posturing. Draco walked up to Jubby, looked him straight in the eye and with audible menace said, "Simon says jump in the pond."

I closed my eyes and sighed. Shit.

I knew my brother better than anybody. There are kids who do not back down from a dare. Jubby would never, *ever* back down from anything. Draco had thrown down the gauntlet. Jumping in the pond was a one-way ticket home. As soon as the challenge was made, I closed my eyes, certain that our ten-year-old asses were headed home. It took my towheaded twin half a second to make his decision, sprint down to the pond, continue his sprint down the long dock and do a friggin' cannonball into the pond. He didn't even think about it. He just did it. Everybody was shocked except me. Like I said, I knew my brother. We're going home. Mom and Dad are getting a call and we're going home.

The Nazis had never seen anything like this. That's the thing about Nazis. Their sense of superiority is their weakness. They don't consider their enemies. When they looked at Jubby, all they saw was a so-called "welly." They didn't know my brother and, therefore, didn't know who the hell they were dealing with. This was a kid who would never give an inch. He would never let anybody be tougher than him.

The cannonball was a perfect ten. His form was pristine, and the splash was perfect. Jubby emerged from the water and pulled himself onto the dock, dripping wet. He marched up the yard and straight at Draco Malfoy. Jubby, drenched in pond water from head to toe, got nose to nose with the little bastard.

"Simon says *kiss my ass.*"

Instant brawl.

Both groups were immediately all over each other. Ten-year-old punches were thrown in every direction. After a minute, the camp counselors materialized having heard the fight. Apparently, a miniature riot was enough to interrupt their reefer session.

"HOLD UP! HOLD UP! WHOA! BREAK IT UP!"

They split us apart from one another. It took quite an effort, I'm sure. Both groups had quickly come to hate the other. They hated us because we looked poor and we hated them for being entitled, arrogant douchebags.

The head counselor was pissed. He was even more upset when he looked over and saw Jubby dripping wet from the pond he'd just jumped into.

"Were you in the pond?"

"No."

"Then why are you wet?"

I was never prouder of my brother than when he gave the coolest answer any ten-year-old ever came up with.

"It's *frickin'* rainng out." (Jubby didn't say 'frickin'')

The counselors couldn't argue with that and they weren't about to challenge it. After all, they weren't exactly doing a great job supervising us in the first place. Also, the vocabulary words we'd learned from our Scout Master Stan finally came in handy. For the first time since being dumped off at this horrible camp, we felt proud of ourselves. We'd stood up to Nazis and made them look bad, but it wasn't over. The counselors, in their stoned brains, thought it would be a good idea to play peacemakers.

"You guys are going to learn to get along."

They pointed at us, "You guys are going to host at your camp site since you have Mount Rushmore. You'll be making Cub Scout dinners for them. By the end of dinner, you little morons are all gonna be best friends. Got it?"

Damn it. There's a lot of things one should never be made to do. Cooking tin foil wrapped pork chops in a campfire for a bunch of Nazis is one of them. Now we were being forced to do just that. We didn't like it, and they weren't going to be able to make us like it. No way. No how. This sucked but there was no getting around it.

That evening the Nazis marched into our camp singing their stupid songs the entire way. "I don't know what I been told. Welfare kids smell like rotten mold." Yep. We were supposed to find a way to become best friends with these a-holes. We ended up grinning and bearing it the best we could. We begrudgingly cooked their stupid meals for them and eventually needed a change of scenery. We grabbed our tinfoil wrapped dinners and climbed to the top of one of the giant rocks to better stomach our food. It's impossible to digest food staring at a group of Hitler Youth.

All my best friends were standing thirty feet atop a giant boulder munching on burned pork chops and admiring the sunset when Draco Malfoy and his group of Nazi henchmen climbed up to join us. Their intent was nefarious. This was a power-play and they were climbing up to antagonize us further. Tension immediately filled the air as Draco started talking trash all over again. That kid just could not shut up. I guess that's just how entitled brats have to act. They just can't bottle up all that anger. We tried to take some kind of high road by ignoring. It wasn't easy, especially for Jubby. I knew he just wanted to pop the kid in the face, and I saw that he was doing everything he could to restrain himself.

He turned his back to the little blonde-haired son-of-a-bitch and stood at the edge of the boulder. Draco, sneaky little puke that he was, saw his chance. I watched in utter disbelief as the sadistic little bastard shoved my brother off the boulder. He Pearl Harbored him! Jubby descended twenty feet into the gnarliest briar patch you can imagine. He initially didn't know what hit him, but he figured it out soon after finding himself swimming in a giant bush of thorns and prickers. Immediately a royal rumble erupted on top of the giant boulder. This was World War III.

When I first took the oath to be a faithful and loyal Cub Scout, I never imagined it would lead to brawling with a bunch of Nazi Youth with my best friends. I was on top of the boulder throwing punches and doing everything I could to fight for the sake of all that is good in the world. So was everyone else in my crew. It might have been a battle fought by kids, but there was something epic about it. This wasn't just rich kids versus poor kids. It felt like good versus evil.

Jubby pulled himself out of the brambles with blood and scrapes covering his arms, legs, and face. He knew who pushed him off the rock. With a look of determination and pure rage he quickly climbed back to the top of the boulder on which a pint-sized Cub Scout vs. Nazi riot had broken out. Jubby found the object of his rage, Draco Malfoy. With brute strength, hyper-charged with rage, he picked Draco up with both hands, lifted him over his head, and threw the little Nazi turd off the boulder into the same pricker bush he just crawled out of. Then to prove alpha dominance, he did something truly unbelievable. My brother amazingly decided to do something no sane person would ever do. Like I said before, the Nazis didn't have a clue who they were messing with. Jubby jumped off the boulder into the briar patch he had thrown his mortal enemy into and continued to beat the ever-living snot out of the kid. Little Hitler needed to learn a lesson and he got it.

I don't remember exactly how the brawl was broken up. I do remember the counselors fuming with rage. They angrily announced that for the rest of the week we were under strict orders not to associate with the other group. We were to be split up at all costs. That was fine with us. Trying to get along with Nazis is an act of stupidity. As far as we were concerned, we had won and were on top of the world. We might have been "the poor kids," but we were rich with something all the other troops didn't have. Sure, they had badges and fancy uniforms and rich parents and all the silver spoons you can imagine. But we had *real* friends, friends who fought *alongside* one another and *for* one another. It would be okay. Nobody could hurt us for the rest of the week.

9

Rock Music Played Backward Is Satan Talking to You

There is no doubt in my mind that music saves lives. Without music I don't know where I'd be and I thank God for its existence every day. Is there anything better than music to help you get through a bad day? I believe the soundtrack of a person's life is more than music, it's their identity. A playlist tells us where we've been, who we are, and where we're headed. Music is one of the reasons I believe in God. How can somebody listen to Beethoven's *Ninth Symphony* or *Hey Jude* and not get a sense of the sublime?

Above almost all things, I love rock music. What's not to love: The Beatles, The Stones, Led Zeppelin, Talking Heads, Pink Floyd, and on and on and on. I'm not a classic rock snob either. I can listen to pop confections like Hall and Oates and one-hit wonders from the 80s all day long. It's the best medicine for just about anything. If you feel down, music lifts you up. If life is great, it provides the perfect melody to accompany your level of joy. I wouldn't say that a life without music wouldn't be worth living, but it might come close.

At eleven years old I was told that rock music was from the Devil. I was also told that listening to it would send me to Hell. Furthermore, I was told that if you played it backwards, it was Lucifer talking to you. My God! How is a kid ever supposed to survive growing up around so much nonsense?

I'm not sure what it says about me that exactly one year after attending a summer camp and fighting a bunch of Hitler youth, I willingly signed up to go to another one. However, this new experience would offer something completely different. I didn't know it at the time, but this camp would be infinitely worse than Cub Scout Camp. This one would threaten me in ways that the Nazis couldn't. This was a camp that would be more akin to a cult as Kool-aid was being stocked and young minds were signing up for indoctrination. It was called "Circle 'C' Camp." The 'C' stood for "Christian."

Just like with Cub Scout Camp, a pamphlet was put in front of me. My friend Raymond, who was not particularly religious, excitedly shoved it in our faces. It had horse-back riding featured on the front and at the top of the advertisement, it just said "Circle 'C' Camp." It looked like an old-west ranch of some sort.

"Do you guys want to go to this camp?"

For some reason, Raymond was pumped up about the idea of spending an entire week riding horses. The pamphlet was selling itself as some kind of Old West joint where kids could learn how to be cowboys and ranch hands. It never even dawned on me to ask what the "C" stood for. It wouldn't have mattered because I wouldn't have known the implications it carried. Had I known, I would have run a mile in the other direction.

Jubby and I thought it looked okay and Raymond seemed excited. We couldn't let him down, so we agreed to go, although I was somewhat reluctant. I didn't like riding horses. To be fair, I actually hated riding horses. The previous few years had seen me get bucked off a cow and two other steeds. We lived in farm country and when you get sick of riding your bike, you and your friends look to other things. We went through a phase where we would find a pasture and hop on the horses, bareback, while the owner of the animals wasn't around. I must have sucked at it. Either that, or horses just didn't like my scrawny butt trying to ride them. They seemed to enjoy bucking me off, though, and I racked up a few concussions along the way. Thank God I'm a country boy!

Just like with Camp Elk Lick, the parents looked the pamphlet over. My mom grew up on a farm and thought it sounded like fun. My father didn't say much but seemed moody about the whole affair. That wasn't unusual, he was moody about almost everything. In the end they agreed to let us go. No begging or pleading was offered, and it turned out none was necessary. They were happy to get rid of us for another week.

From the get-go, I think I had a bad feeling about things. It was like a premonition. It may have been residual emotions from the bad experience of the previous summer camp, but I had a mild feeling that this place wasn't going to be good for me. I wouldn't belong there. Somehow, I just knew it. Incidentally, there was one major sign that should have been somewhat of a tip-off. After signing up and sending some money to secure our spots, we received a flyer in the mail. It gave us a heads-up about all the camp rules and expectations.

The thing that jumped out to me most was the dress code. What a pain in the neck. In reading the paragraph about clothing regulations, I realized I might be in trouble.

ABSOLUTELY NO ROCK BAND T-SHIRTS WILL BE WORN.

Crap. Just about every single T-shirt I owned had Led Zeppelin, AC/DC, The Rolling Stones, or Pink Floyd, logos on them. We had to make a quick trip to the store to buy a week's supply of white T-shirts. Why would this camp have a problem with rock T-shirts? I didn't know and for some reason, I didn't ask. I must have figured they just wanted it to seem like the Old West or something. Either way, I remember wondering if Wyatt Earp and Doc Holiday were wandering around Tombstone wearing white T-shirts their moms had bought them from JC Penney.

On the drive to the camp everything seemed fine. My mercurial father was in a pissy mood, but that was normal, and my mother was quiet. It seemed like they had been fighting because there was an uncomfortable tension in the car. We rolled through the gates of the camp and before long we were meeting our counselor. His name was Randy. He was one of the gawkiest and gangliest guys I'd ever seen. Randy was roughly twenty-one years old and he was all knees and elbows. Looking at his face was like looking into two miniature fish-tanks because the poor guy had some serious Coke-bottle glasses. Randy's most notable feature, though, was his mullet. It was one of the best mullets I'd ever seen. It was impressive. Seriously. It looked like a well-brushed horse's mane. In the eighties the mullet hairstyle held status. It would be mocked by people in the more enlightened future, but in its day it was majestic. You could tell that Randy's coiffure made him feel like the king of the camp.

My parents eventually vanished and returned home to a peaceful week without our presence. Curiously, they didn't seem to want to stick around too long. My father was noticeably itching to leave as soon as possible. We entered our new home. It was a small cabin with two bunk beds in it. Nothing special at all. Randy was our personal counselor, so he was supposed to bunk with us and be our guide through everything. He was super-excited and it made me nervous. I was still a little gun shy about counselors from my Cub Scout Camp experience, but Randy seemed different. He looked weird but it seemed like he really liked us and was going to be a good guy. He was giving off an "I'm your new big brother" kind of vibe.

When we were done putting our clothes away, Randy had each of us fill out a questionnaire that asked our likes and dislikes and stuff like that. When we finished, he collected the forms and then sat us on the bunks to have our first little pow wow of the camp. His voice took on a curious tone I'd never heard before. First, he had a southern accent, but all of the sudden he also sounded terribly worried. His voice came across like an overly concerned mom who just can't tell you *how very much she truly, truly loves you.*

"I am so blessed. I am blessed to be given a chance to get to know you guys. We're gonna have such a great time this week. It's gonna be so radical. I can already tell you guys seem like such rad little dudes. We're going to get really, really close this week…like a family."

Oh, no. We all looked at each other with the same thought. Maybe Randy was a god-damned child molester. It would turn out he wasn't, at least I don't think he was. We would learn that Randy was not interested in our bodies. Nope, good old Randy was interested in way more than that…Randy was interested in our souls.

"We're going to have some real adventures and we're going to face some very serious challenges. There's gonna be times this week when you guys are going to have to be strong. You'll have to dig down deep and find strength you never knew you had. It's gonna be super important that I know what makes you guys tick. I gotta know who you are, what your fears are, your goals, your interests, who you want to be when you grow up, but most of all I want to know what *Jesus* means to you."

And there it was. Jesus. Riding horses, it turned out, was far down on the agenda of stuff to do at Circle 'C' Camp. It was a classic bait and switch scenario. This was a camp that's singular purpose was to whore out the idea of cowboy adventures just so it could get down to selling some good-old fashioned Jesus juice. It was Randy's job to get us as thirsty as possible.

The ink was still fresh on the questionnaires we had just filled out when Randy started to look them over to see what "made us guys tick." He got to mine and looked up from my survey with raised eyebrows. I became nervous. Randy glared at me through his giant glasses with a strange expression that I couldn't interpret.

"Dude. You *really* like these bands. Come on, man. *Seriously*?"

One of the questions asked was what my "likes" were and I decided to write down a few of my favorite musical artists.

"Yeah."

I loved my music. Maybe Randy was a fellow music lover.

"You actually like The Rolling Stones…Mick Jagger?"

"Definitely."

In my book guys like Mick Jagger and Robert Plant were rock gods.

"Doesn't it bother you that Mick Jagger works for Satan?"

Hold the phone. What the hell is this googly eyed freak talking about!!???

"Uhhhhh"

"I'm serious, little buddy. I've done some major study of this stuff. Don't you know that all these bands are linked to the Devil?"

Get the hell out of here. Who the hell does Randy think he is! My mind is racing a mile a minute and I can feel my heart beating. I'm not sure whether to be pissed off that my sacred music was under attack or to storm out of the cabin because my counselor was a nut-job. I'm shy by nature and not one to argue. So, I sit and listen to this spectacled weirdo. I listen for the next half hour as Randy gave his doctoral thesis on how Satan invented rock music to seduce young minds and get legions of would-be Devil worshipers to join him in Hell for all eternity. Randy's not messing around. This dude is as serious as a heart attack. And then comes the thing that seals the deal. It's the ace up the sleeve. This is Randy's big moment and, boy, is he prepared. Wait for it…

"Do you know if you play rock music backwards, it's the Devil talking to you?"

"Whaaaat?"

We'd never heard anything like this.

"I'm serious and if you don't believe me, I've got tapes. I can show you some of the hidden messages Satan has planted in certain songs."

Suddenly a little boom box is brought out with a case of TDK cassette tapes with hand-written labels on them. Randy starts pawing through them until he finds the right one.

"Aha! Here it is. You guys just wait until you hear this."

His excitement is beyond belief. He was in the process of saving our souls! This is what God put him on the planet to do and nothing could be more important than being the Lord's warrior at this very moment. You go, Randy!

"Check this out little dudes."

Randy pops the tape in and presses play. For the next half hour, we listened to the stupidest thing I'd ever heard. Garbled, muffled, warped, bizarre sounds of music hissed and groaned at us. We sat on the bunks and listened for what seemed like an eternity. We listened to an entire three-minute-long song…being played in reverse. When it was over, we sat in befuddlement with baffled looks on our faces.

Randy cuts through the silence, "Did you hear that?"

The look on his face showed that he was convinced he was reaching us. But he still had doubts. He'd have to work harder to save our heathen rock and roll listening souls.

"So that was Elvis Presley's 'Heartbreak Hotel'"

Silence.

"Elvis Presley, the so-called 'King of Rock and Roll' is a messenger of Satan. You listened to the music backwards. Did you hear anything funny?"

Silence.

"Let me play it for you again."

He did.

Three minutes later, Randy stops the tape in excitement.

"See! Did you guys hear it? It's unmistakable. It said, 'the Devil is your friend.' Did you hear it…undeniable."

Wow! This dude had conviction. And he wasn't done.

"Do you guys know what eternity is?"

"It means forever, right?"

"Yep."

Our new counselor decides to take a long and dramatic pause. Imagine Randy staring off into space for a few seconds.

"Forever. Think about it, guys. *Forever*. You can't even wrap your minds around the concept of forever, right? That's eternity."

"Next question: Have you guys ever gotten burned by fire?"

"Oh, yeah…this one time…"

Randy cuts us off, "It's painful, right? Really painful." Another dramatic pause.

"Imagine the pain of that burn all over your entire body…. for eternity. I don't know about you guys, but I'm positive about one thing for myself. I wouldn't want to burn in the fires of Hell for all eternity just because I listened to some Mick Jagger music."

Randy drops the frickin' mic and walks out.

We sat dumbfounded. The Catholic Church certainly had a grip on me, but this was some next-level stuff going on. I didn't know what to think. None of us did. The indoctrination process had officially begun.

When I think back, it was truly impressive how little we rode horses that week. That pamphlet was full of crap. Another case of false advertising to kids. Honestly, I wasn't terribly upset about the lack of equestrian play time. I didn't want to ride horses in the first place. No, I was super pissed about something else, and I wasn't sure I'd ever forgive Raymond for getting us into this entire mess. You see, according to the camp schedule, we were required to go to "Chapel" not once, not twice, not three times, but four times every! single! day! Agonizing. I'd like to think that Jesus, having experienced a fair amount of pain, would think going to church that many times in a day was cruel and unusual punishment. I, for one, didn't go to summer camp to overdose on church.

This Chapel experience taught me some new things. One thing I learned was a *new* form of intolerance: Religious discrimination. It turned out that Jubby and I were the only Catholic kids at Circle 'C' Camp. The "C" stood for

Christian, but it was definitely leaning hard toward a Protestant denomination of some sort. We soon found out that Catholics were not "Christian" in their view. That was news to us. I guess they weren't really history buffs. It's not like they treated us like lepers upon finding out we were Catholic. They kind of just seemed awkward around us after finding out…like they didn't know how to talk to us. "The Catholic kids" was what they called us. It wasn't exactly derogatory, but it felt judgmental. When they referred to us that way, it was with a tone of pity. We found ourselves playing the role of "the other." We were "the kids whose beliefs are wrong." We were outsiders who didn't belong and if we told other campers we were Catholic, they'd ask, "So, you're not Christian, then?" We just shrugged and went along with things. That's the safest thing to do where indoctrination is concerned.

The Chapel experience was shocking to us. It was different than the Catholic masses we were used to in almost every way. Those kids were feeling something I'd never seen people in church feel before. They were into it. There were all sorts of things going on I'd never seen. Kids were singing and feeling the power of the Lord and crying. There was a lot of crying. People would be on their knees singing and weeping and praying. It was a spectacle. There was lots of hugging and it made me uncomfortable. Jubby felt the same way. We just watched with our mouths open. Our church wasn't like this at all.

Four times a day I was in awe of this spectacle, but I wasn't bored. I was a little freaked out, and too busy questioning my Catholic beliefs to be bored. There was also a game they would play in every Chapel session. They would interrupt the singing, praying, hugging, crying routine with this thing they called "Sword Competition." This was something Jubby and I had never experienced. Catholic kids don't really read the Bible. You might have it read to you, but you don't do a heck of a lot of in-depth Bible study growing up Catholic. You just absorb the priests take on things from the Homily and go about your way. "Sword Competitions" would be a particular challenge for two kids who literally didn't know the difference between *Genesis* and *Leviticus*. The game involved somebody at the podium calling out a random Book, Chapter, and Verse in the Bible as if they were running a Bingo Hall. Then the room would erupt into a mad fury of little fingers flipping through Bible pages. The fingers would be like hurricanes as the children focused intently on the task at hand. The kid who found the right Book, Chapter, and Verse would then raise his hand high in the air and yell out the verse as loudly and passionately as he could.

"LET THERE BE LIGHT AND THERE WAS LIGHT!"

We were outmatched. Chapel went on four times a day for a week and not once was either one of us quick enough to call out an answer. It was obvious that all these other boys and girls had downed the Kool-Aid a long time ago and were little Bible reading maniacs. Here Jubby and I were struggling to figure out what the hell a *Deuteronomy* was while everyone else was pulling quotes from the Good Book out of their assess at light speed. It was difficult for me as I didn't know anything about the Bible. It was five times more difficult for Jubby who was terribly dyslexic. Either way, the horses outside the chapel remained largely unridden as we continued the much more important journey of having our souls saved.

That was the big word throughout the entire week. *Saved.* Salvation. Being saved by Jesus. Being saved in the eyes of the Lord. People kept asking us if we'd been saved.

"Have you been saved by Jesus?"

"Have you accepted Jesus into your hearts?"

It was asked all the time and it freaked me out because I didn't really know what it meant. How was I supposed to respond? Campers would reminisce about the first time they were saved. They would talk about the "Saving Ceremonies" they had been a part of at other camps. These kids would brag about how many times they'd been saved in the same way other kids might brag about how many times they rode a roller-coaster.

"How did you feel the first time you were saved?"

"It was like seeing light for the first time."

"I never knew such love could be possible."

"My third time was the best."

"Nothing is ever like the first time."

Wow. Getting saved sure sounded like a big deal. I hadn't been saved and I was a little afraid. Questions flooded into my young mind. Do my parents know about this "saving" stuff? If so, why haven't they told us about it? Would they want us to be saved? Are we going to Hell if we aren't saved? Are mom and dad going to be pissed if we get saved? I had zero answers to any of these questions and cognitive dissonance was splitting my little brain in two.

In retrospect, there was no ill-intent at work. It was just garden variety indoctrination, and I was too naïve to see through it. It was effective though. I never fully drank the Kool-Aid, but my mind was being bent and my world view was being shaken. I wasn't old enough or wise enough to effectively analyze what was happening. Jubby and I were just bewildered. We asked each other a lot of questions that week. This camp was doing something to us, it was making us doubt who we were. Much about the Catholic beliefs we had grown up with was being challenged. At the time I didn't know much about theology and other people's views of God. I had questions. Who was right? Who was wrong? What am I supposed to believe? If I choose the wrong belief, am I going to Hell? The more I thought about it, the more confused I became. The intensity of the worshipers at Chapel *must* mean something. All those people hugging and crying! I'd never seen such passion in a church. They must have a secret knowledge that I don't. But, what about being Catholic? My mind was spinning.

The final night of camp was built up all week long. It was the main event. They had organized it to be an epic saving ceremony and the owner was supposed to grace the camp with his presence that evening. I guess he liked to hide out of sight until the grand finale. He was not only the owner but a pastor as well. Apparently, he was a legend in the minds of the campers. They talked him up all week as though he were some kind of Yoda-like figure. They called him "Master Pastor."

When the final night arrived, the entire camp was gathered in the large chapel. I'd logged quite a few hours in that place over the course of the week. We had been through a lot of prayer services and our minds were spinning with all sorts of new thoughts. I stood in the middle of the church with nothing but confusion. Worse, I was surrounded by people who had absolute conviction in their beliefs. I looked from one wide-eyed face to another and knew one thing for sure, I wasn't sharing the same feelings. Then, suddenly, the counselors' faces were struck with awe. The room became silent. The owner had arrived.

"Ladies and Gentlemen…behold…Master Pastor!"

Deafening applause erupted throughout the room as Master Pastor entered the building. He wasn't what I expected. They had built him up to be like a god, but my first impression was of an old snapping turtle. He had a mean, distrusting look to him. He wore a cowboy hat and a Texas string tie. To this day, that is a look that sends shivers down my spine. His movements were turtle-like as well. Not slow, just deliberate and awkward as he shuffled down the aisle towards the stage to take a seat on his throne. The applause subsided and a brief but overwhelmingly emotional speech was made by the head counselor. He wanted to get the congregation riled up for the big soul-saving moment. It was going to be a mass saving. All souls must go to Heaven. The counselor really gave it his all. His goal was to stoke the flames of passion in the young hearts of the congregation, and he was doing a fantastic job.

Kids began fainting, really. Jubby and I couldn't believe our eyes. It was like they were possessed. I'd never felt more self-conscious in my life. Everybody else was feeling something powerful and we were just standing with our mouths open at the spectacle. Truthfully, I was terrified. What were we supposed to do? Fake it?

Our twin power kicked in again and an intuitive decision was made. We knew we had to go along with it. God knows what they would do to us if we didn't blend in. Hell, for all we knew, they might sacrifice us to Jesus and then eat us afterward. I saw *Children of the Corn.* Maybe this would be like that. Who knew?

Suddenly we found ourselves in a line moving toward the old turtle in the cowboy hat. You couldn't really make out what was going on at the front of the church, but you could tell it was some kind of ruckus. Every few seconds the group in front of Master Pastor would cheer in excitement…as if they had witnessed a miracle. All over the room, people would be dancing around with hands in the air and throwing fits. We couldn't make it out because there was too large a crowd blocking the view. As we got closer and closer I was feeling more anxiety than I'd ever felt. I was going to be *saved* and I still had no idea what it meant. Once I was saved, would I be different? Would the world be more colorful? Would I know love for the first time? Would I not go to Hell now? Would I still be me? What would happen to the old me? Was I betraying my Catholic upbringing? Would my parents approve of this? I was being herded toward a transformation.

Jubby, Raymond and I finally arrived at the front of the chapel and found oursleves standing face to face with the wrinkly old man who was responsible for this entire show. My heart was beating out of my chest.

Jubby was first. With trepidation, he stepped in front of that old snapper.

"Do you love Jesus Christ the Lord as your savior and reject Satan and all his minions of evil?"

"Uhhhhh…. Yes?"

Turtle-man took the palm of his wrinkly old hand, cupped my brother's face in it and threw him backward. Jubby fell into two counselors who caught him and stood him back up. Jubby looked at me with a quizzical expression. I didn't need twin powers to understand. It clearly said, "What the hell was that?" He just got saved. Is he still Jubby? Is he still my brother?

I felt like running out of the building with my hair on fire but there was no escape. Jubby had just been saved and now it was my turn. I got the same routine, the same question, the same answer, the same boink to the head, the fall, and being propped back up. It was terrifying and embarrassing the entire time. I hated every minute of it. What I hated most was I wasn't there by choice. I was like a cow being herded to some kind of slaughter. The influence of lining up and following the herd had control of me. I was powerless against it. Non-participation didn't feel like it was an option. They wouldn't have let you sit this out. Throughout the entire process I felt nothing spiritual or religious. Other kids were speaking in tongues and having the Holy Spirit make them do all kinds of crazy stuff and I couldn't wait for it to be over. What was wrong with me?

The three of us walked back to our seats as the congregation continued in a bedlam of song and tears and hugging. They were possessed by spiritual ecstasy. Random kids were embracing us with tears in their eyes and telling us how proud they were that we'd finally found Jesus.

"You're one of us now."

There was just an overwhelming feeling of discomfort. We had not been transformed and we didn't feel any different, just more confused. And we still had so much confusion and so many questions. Mostly, we felt like something must be wrong with us. Was it our fault? How is everyone else so profoundly moved when we were not?

"Do you feel different?" I whispered to Jubby.

"Nope. You?"

"I don't think so."

We walked through the summer night from the chapel to our cabin in silence. I looked up at the stars trying to comprehend God and the mysteries of the vast universe. I did not come to summer camp to face this kind of bewilderment. I needed answers. This was beyond my comprehension.

We woke up the next morning and the entire camp was glowing from the previous night's mass saving ceremony. Everyone continued to hug and cry while the three of us didn't know how to feel or what to do. None of us were huggers but good old Randy sure was. He was super-excited and stoked that he'd played some part in saving our souls. He made me promise that I would go home and burn all my Mick Jagger albums. Randy had done his job like a good Christian warrior. As far as he was concerned, the backward music tapes had worked and he was a hero.

Finally, my parents showed up, hastily stuffed us in the family car and headed home. Immediately, there was palpable tension as we drove down the road. My father was not talking. In fact, Captain Catholic seemed sort of pissed. When my old man was silent, that usually meant trouble. It was a "calm before a storm" kind of thing. My mother was also very quiet. They'd obviously been fighting before arriving to pick us up. Jubby and I weren't oblivious, we just had bigger fish to fry. Something inside us felt urgent and we were itching to ask them an important question. Hell, it was beyond urgent, it was imperative, and had to be asked right away. A concern had been planted inside us. We needed to spread the word and the word had to be spread by asking the question that was on our minds. Sitting in the back of the car with nothing but silence, Jubby and I locked eyes. Our telepathic twin power kicked in. I read his mind.

Are you gonna ask?

He read mine back.

I'm scared. You ask.

His mind replied.

Okay.

Jubby, always the braver one, finally piped up.

"Mom…Dad…Ummmm…"

There was a pause. He looked at me. The intentness in my face must have given him the resolve he needed.

"Have you guys accepted Jesus as your savior and would you be willing to be saved so that your souls won't burn in Hell for eternity?"

Screeeech. The car slammed to a stop. It was exactly the wrong question to ask at that very moment. My Catholic father, who never wanted us at this camp for fear of being brainwashed by Protestants, turned from the wheel and looked at his newly saved sons sitting in the backseat. With rage in his eyes he pointed his finger down at us.

"You two were saved when you were frickin' (he didn't say 'frickin') baptized in the Catholic Church. I don't ever want to hear any more of that Protestant crap!"

He violently shoved the gears back into Drive and we headed home in silence.

I had questions and my head was swimming with confusion. What was the big deal? Why did my father not like Protestants? Was being saved a bad thing? Was I going to Hell? Who am I supposed to believe? I was owed an explanation. We drove straight to the Church Rectory and didn't even stop home first. My father knocked on the priest's door and proceeded to tell him about our experience from the previous week. Father Francis was amused and was more than happy to bend our minds to being Catholic again. There was an hour-long chat and then we headed to the church for Confession to hit the reset button.

After telling the priest my sins, I had an important question to ask. It was really bothering me.

"Father…can I still listen to The Rolling Stones?"

"Don't be stupid. Of course."

Thank God. I was saved.

10

Burning Down the Pool

"Why can't we have anything nice?"

I would lay a bet that, over the course of twenty years, my father said these exact words over a thousand times. The cause was simple, he had three sons who broke a lot of his possessions. We got so used to hearing him ask the question, "Why can't we have anything nice?" we could almost set our watches by it. We would know almost exactly when he would say it, you could feel it coming. He always said it the same way, too. His voice held a mixture of exasperation and simmering anger. The tone of his words would hint at a notion that he regretted siring three sons who had zero regard for maintaining the quality of material possessions, whatever they may be.

I had to feel sorry for my old man. His question was valid. "Why can't we have anything nice?" My parents worked hard and tried to provide nice things. As high school teachers, they were far from rich, but they busted their assess day in and day out to provide for us. We had a nice house, we always had two cars, we had toys, they tried to get nice furniture, a nice stereo, nice wallpaper, nice beds, nice curtains, nice carpeting, etc. Despite all their efforts to provide these "nice" things, their sons had an uncanny knack for damaging them. I'm sure it must have seemed, to my parents, like we were doing it deliberately. Sometimes my father's oft-repeated question would be followed with another inquiry.

"What the hell is wrong with you?"

It wasn't so much a question as much as an accusation. We knew what we were being accused of. We were guilty of one simple thing…not using our heads. It was a statement that immediately cut you down and made you feel stupid. You couldn't really answer it either. Obviously, something was wrong with you. Otherwise, you wouldn't keep "accidentally" destroying your parents' things. The question would be repeated, too.

"What the hell is wrong with you?"

This time the inquiry came with more volume and demanded an answer. Invariably, there wasn't one available, just silence. The only thing you could do was hang your head and look ashamed of yourself. "What the hell is wrong with you?" is a question that will get any kid well-associated with the look of his sneakers.

"Shame on you. Use your head next time."

I honestly think we tried. But stuff just had a way of getting destroyed despite our best efforts.

Childhood isn't for the faint of heart. Irony, dramatic tension, and tragedy aren't just for theatrical stages. Real life is its own Greek tragedy and we are all victims of circumstance. This is particularly true when you're a kid. Things can just go terribly wrong sometimes. When I look back at some events, it seems like the cruel hand of fate was playing its part and the memory remains vivid due to the emotional residue. The summer before I went into sixth grade was such a doozy that it almost ripped my family apart. Two epic calamities would test the fabric that loosely held us together and would drive my father beyond his breaking point. The entire question of "Why can't we have anything nice?" would be pushed to a its ultimate limit.

There were two events that summer that none of us would ever forget, especially my twin brother, who at the age of nine was already legendary for his destructive acumen. He was truly a Rembrandt when it came to messing things up; it was amazing. He was like King Midas, except whatever he touched, instead of turning to gold, would just fall apart. He didn't mean to break stuff, it just kind of happened. It got to a point where he felt he was cursed, maybe he was.

As I mentioned, that summer was a doozy, and two separate catastrophes were about to take place that would change all of us forever. Jubby, my poor twin brother, would be defined and haunted by these events for years to come. Both occurrences would threaten to prove, without the shadow of a doubt, that my father might never be able to have anything nice.

The summer started with the most exciting thing a kid could imagine. My parents had somehow saved up enough money to install an in-ground pool in our backyard. It was like Christmas in June. The construction of the pool was unbelievable. It was unreal. How the hell were *we*, of all people, getting a pool? None of us had ever been so excited. Jubby and I were doing everything we could to speed up the process. It couldn't happen fast enough. We were offering to help the workers with the installation. The pool guys, seeing how eager we were, would give us little jobs. They must have gotten a kick out of our desperation and were more than willing to let us give them a hand. Heck, we were so pumped to get a pool we would have built the whole damn thing ourselves if we knew how.

Weeks went by testing the patience of two ten-year old kids. Slowly but surely a huge muddy pit eventually became a brand-new glistening oasis. It was the whole nine yards, too. Full size. Shallow end. Deep end. Twisty, blue slide. Diving board. Cement patio. It was surrounded by a six-foot tall wooden fence. It wasn't just a pool, it was an aquatic heaven, and it was ours. Our lives were perfect; we were going to have a place to swim, forever! Jubby and I had constant arguments as to who was going to be the first one in the pool, an honor that would be held for all time. It wouldn't matter. Nothing mattered. We had zero cares. We knew only one thing: It wasn't going to get any better than this!

Unfortunately, we were flying too close to the sun. We would learn the danger of feeling that life was perfect. While the pool was being constructed, we had been in a perpetual state of excitement. Helping the workers could only distract us for so long and we had too much pent-up energy that needed to be channeled. It felt like we were going to go crazy with all the waiting. There was simply too much time before the pool was complete. It was imperative that we distract ourselves and spend our energy in another way. We figured that playing a lot of basketball was the best way to kill time before we could start launching cannonballs into our new pool. My parents owned a two-car garage that was detached from the house. There was a cement driveway that acted as our basketball court. A hoop and backboard were mounted on the front of the garage enabling us to play ball any time we wanted. It was a pretty typical American dream set-up. There was even a white picket fence involved. Jubby and I loved playing basketball and took every chance we could to shoot hoops. While the days of the calendar were being crossed off until the pool was ready, we were spending all our time playing one-on-one and perfecting our jump shots.

At ten years old, we had somehow persuaded my mother to let us drive her car. Well, that's not completely accurate. We'd convinced her to let us back the car out of the garage and put it in park at the far end of the driveway. Because the garage was always a mess and full of lots of junk, the small sedan would always be half-in and half out of the garage, making it difficult to shoot hoops. The only solution: Back that thing up. My busy mother must have gotten sick of us asking her if she'd move the car so we could shoot baskets. Without con-cern, she just started throwing us her keys and allowing us to do it ourselves.

"Just back it up and leave it at the end of the drive."

It's amazing, with our history of destruction, she would allow this. My mother was a sensible woman who neither drank nor gambled. Maybe allowing a mere child to operate a moving vehicle in reverse was her way of putting some excitement into her life. I'm not sure if my old man knew about it, probably not. Regardless, it just became a ritual. Jubby would say, "Mom, throw me the keys." The car would then be backed up by a boy barely old enough to see above the dashboard. Hoops would be played, no problem. This was the routine and it seemed fine at the time. We never imagined that anything bad would happen until a fateful day, while the pool was being built, when all hell broke loose.

On this day I challenged Jubby to a game of H-O-R-S-E and the challenge was accepted. There was one problem, the Chevy Prism was in the way. The front end was in the garage and the ass-end was hanging out of the bay. Quick as a wink, Jubby goes inside to get the keys and before you can say Kareem-Abdul-Jabbar, he's sitting in the light blue four door, starting the engine. I'm standing on the cement pad with a green and white Boston Celtics basketball in my hands looking on. Jubby begins backing up. He didn't exactly floor it but he was reversing at a rapid pace which would have been fine, except for one thing. He had forgotten to shut the driver's side door before backing up. Like many two car garages, the two bays in our garage were separated from one another by a dividing wall. If one were to look at the façade, they'd see two separate openings divided by a little section of siding. It goes without saying that it would be very important to make sure a car door is fully closed while backing out.

Sometimes life can go into slow motion. This was one of those moments. I looked on as the very open driver's side door made an impact with the very immovable dividing wall. The glass from the door's window exploded into a billion glistening pieces and scattered like diamonds over the cement. The corresponding sound of bending metal was terrifying. The door bent all the way to the front panel of the car while the hinges bent beyond their limit. The door was now hugging the driver's-side wheel. Time, that was moving in that terrible slow motion, suddenly froze and the planet stopped rotating for a few seconds. The explosion of noise and glass was over and now there was only silence.

"Holy shit." I dropped the basketball.

Slowly, Jubby got out of the destroyed car with an expression on his face I'd never really seen. It was beyond fear, it was sick. His mouth was open and unable to form words. He couldn't have said anything if he wanted to, panic was gripping his throat. It was a face that wanted three seconds back so he could close that door and back the car up properly. It was a face that knew the tragic impossibility of being able to relive those few seconds and spare himself the wrath of our enraged father. Hell, enraged wasn't the right word. My dad got enraged when he found that one of his dipshit sons had accidentally scratched one of his record albums. This would be infinitely worse. This would be enraged times a thousand. It was unimaginable how unbelievably pissed the old man would be when he saw that his ten-year-old son had wrecked the car.

It was not my best moment. Every shred of brotherly loyalty left me.

"You're screwed."

I was not getting any blame for this. This was not my fault. I wanted nothing to do with it. He wrecked the car, not me. I wasn't about to take any heat or share any blame for something as bad as this. Like a coward, I ran from the glass-filled cement into the house. I grabbed some snacks, hustled up to my room, grabbed an ass-load of comic books and hid under my bed. It was going to be a long day and, although I felt very scared for my brother, I wasn't about to hang around to see what was going to happen. I know in the military they say to "never leave a man behind." That day I was guilty as charged for leaving not a man, but my twin brother behind.

It sure didn't take long for the brown and sticky stuff to hit the fan. When he found out that his car had been destroyed, my father lost his mind in a way I'd never experienced before. To be fair, I didn't see it. I was under my bed, cowering, but I heard everything. I'm sure the entire neighborhood heard it. My old man lit into my poor brother with an eruption of swear-words that were foreign to me up until that moment. It was an epic reaming out that lasted over an hour. I'm sure Jubby was staring at his Nikes the entire time.

When the rant finally ended, my father made his youngest son ride in the passenger seat of the car he'd just destroyed while the old man drove to the mechanic's shop. I remember looking out the window and seeing the bizarre sight of the damaged car zooming up the road. Jubby was staring straight ahead, half in shame and half in shock while my father, looking angrier than I'd ever seen him, was driving with one hand on the wheel and his left arm holding the mangled door to the car. The force of the collision had bent the driver's door beyond its original size and therefore wouldn't be able to close without the help of a darn good collision guy. I feared I'd never see my brother again. My father wasn't above driving him a few hundred miles away and leaving him on the side of the road. I'm positive he had made that exact threat during his hour-long rant. There was no reason for Jubby not to believe this was a possibility.

Luckily that didn't happen but when they returned, the drama continued. My mother attempted to come to Jubby's rescue and gave the "It was an accident" defense to stick up for her son. Jubby was beyond repentant, but my father just kept repeating, "Why can't we have anything nice?" This eventually escalated to one of those epic fights where the kids are told to go to their rooms only to hear an argument leading them to wonder if mom and dad would be getting a divorce. Dishes were thrown and could be heard smashing against the wall. I'm glad I didn't see this battle firsthand; we had taken refuge in our bedrooms and could only listen.

Eventually, the family went to sleep that night feeling that our household was on shaky ground. The next morning, the smoke had cleared a little, but we were still uneasy and walked on eggshells. It would take time for things to go back to normal. You go day to day hoping the icky feeling of discomfort and unease goes away. Thankfully the divorce wouldn't happen, but there was a lasting tension in the air that could be felt for weeks. Jubby would face no real punishment for the crime he had accidentally committed, shame was enough. He would neither want to play basketball nor back a car out of the garage for a long time. Eventually the car came back all fixed up like brand new. Before long, even though it wasn't forgotten, the event was mostly behind us. In fact, it wasn't that hard to move on because we had better days ahead of us. It was summer and school was over. Most importantly, we had the most amazing thing to look forward to, the pool.

Finally, the brand-new swimming pool had been completed and was ready to be used. It would only be a matter of time before Jubby and I would be doing jack-knifes and backflips off the diving board, jumping off the ten-foot-tall slide, and playing endless amounts of Marco Polo with our friends. To top it all off, it was *ours*, and it was pristine. It wasn't somebody else's pool that you'd have to ask permission to swim in. No, it was ours and we could swim in it any time we damn well felt like it. Everything about it was new and perfect because the construction guys were artists. It was a ten-foot-deep masterpiece. The ceiling of the Sistine Chapel didn't have anything on this aquatic work of art. The patterned rubber blue liner was the bluest thing I'd ever seen. The way that the summer sun bounced off the water made it feel unreal. The cement patio framed the entire oval majestically. The water was as clear as crystal. Birds rested on the fence and admired its beauty. When you opened the gate, you could almost hear a chorus of soprano angels in heaven singing its praise. "Ahhhhhhhhhhhhhhhh." All of us just shared the same feeling. We felt lucky. How did we deserve to have this masterpiece in our backyard?

My father loved to talk about the pool with his friends. He had a right to be proud. He'd invite people over for a drink to beam about his beautiful accomplishment. "You've got to come over and enjoy a Martini with me poolside." Like his sons, my father also felt lucky to have something this nice, hell, it was beyond nice. He had worked hard all his life to afford this luxury and deserved to be proud of the achievement. It was perfect but perfection can't last forever. One day, a few weeks into the summer, our feeling of being lucky came to a grinding halt. An event was about to occur that would challenge everything.

The old man liked to take walks in those days and his daily stroll usually happened in the evenings. He would follow a path leading out of the town onto a gravel country road following alongside the river. My father, famous for serious paranoia and intense hypochondria, would grab a cane that concealed a sword inside it. A little Derringer pistol was also concealed in his pocket. He was afraid of being attacked by rabid dogs he imagined roaming the neighborhoods. He often told us to look out for these vicious pooches when riding our bikes around town. Sometimes he would enjoy a little company and ask one of us to go on his walk with him. It was father-son bonding and I always enjoyed these moments. My father, being an English teacher, would use the opportunity to talk about great books. I would be walking with him along the river as he talked of Huckleberry Finn and Jim on a raft traveling down the Mississippi. My mind would be enthralled.

I was up in my bedroom half-way through a Spider-Man comic book when my father called up the stairs.

"Does anybody want to go for a walk with me?"

"Sure," I called out.

I always liked accompanying him on these excursions but there was another reason I wanted to go. My role in the family had always been that of peacekeeper. More than anyone else in our tribe, I was keenly aware when someone's orbs were out of orbit. I didn't like people to be unhappy or upset so I would take it upon myself to smooth things over. It was an aspect of my personality that would be a defining characteristic my entire life. Even though we had a new pool to make life more amazing than I'd ever dreamed, I was still worried. As I said, there was a lasting tension and the family turmoil gave me a ton of anxiety. After the car door incident, I took any moment that presented itself to make my father a little happier and a leisurely stroll with the old man was just the ticket.

He was already armed with a miniature pistol and sword-cane when I met him at the porch. We were prepared to murder a rabid poodle if the need arose.

"Let's go."

There was no way of knowing that in between the time we left and the time we returned our world would undergo a seismic shift, a shift that would, for better or worse, be a defining moment for all of us. This was going to be a day that would "live in infamy" for the family history books.

It was a perfect summer night, calm and peaceful. Early summer always has a special feeling to it, like there is so much possibility. The future seems so bright. I remember thinking that my father finally seemed as though he had moved on from the destroyed car. We, as a family, had rounded a corner. There was a sense of relief that things were back to normal and the tension from the car incident was finally over.

My God, how wrong I would be.

After walking about three miles down the road, we turned around and started for home. When we reached a mile away from our house, we saw a strange sight. An eleven-year-old boy was peddling on a bicycle in our direction. When the kid got closer, I realized it was Jubby. He wasn't just peddling; the kid was pumping his little legs like he was on the last stretch of the Tour de France. If you looked up from the furious cycling of his feet, you would have seen an ashen face, a face of terror.

"Hey Jubby," my father said.

No response. My brother only peddled more furiously and sped right by us. He didn't look at us. He didn't say anything. Jubby just stared straight ahead and peddled. I turned to look after him as he sped down the road and disappeared over the horizon. How bizarre, something must be wrong. He didn't stop, didn't talk to us, didn't even look at us. I also noticed he was wearing a backpack. My father didn't seem too disturbed by it, though. Weird crap was always happening in my family.

"Huh. He must have left something in the woods."

I agreed with my dad.

"Yeah, probably," I said trying to hide my worry.

I had a sinking feeling that something was terribly wrong. My twin power was tingling. In retrospect, I may have been absorbing some of the anxiety my brother was feeling. I quietly continued walking next to my father, but my mind was occupied. What did Jubby do? Something must be wrong. Eventually, we made it home and my old man announced that he would be out at the pool relaxing with a Martini.

"What are you going to do?" He asked me.

"I guess I'm gonna go back up to my room to read some comics."

"Okay."

Approximately five minutes went by. I grabbed the Spider-Man comic I had been reading, flopped on my bed and jumped back into the world of comic book fiction that insulated me from real life. Then, through my open window, I heard yelling from the pool yard. It wasn't just yelling, though. It was unfettered, unadulterated, pure, not appropriate for young ears profanity. I'd heard my father swear before, but this was something else. This was uncontrolled rage. No, it wasn't rage. Rage is what somebody might have after their son breaks the door from the family car. This was a nuclear fury. My father was furious and the words that were coming out of his mouth were terrifying.

It would be impossible to hide under my bed this time. I had to see what was going on. I had done the math and it was apparent that Jubby had done something unimaginable. Why was my brother furiously peddling by us with a backpack on? My father had gone to the pool. Something must be wrong with the pool. Jubby must have done something awful. But, what? That was the burning question.

I ran out to find my father in a ballistic rage. His face was as red as a tomato and he was screaming obscenities for the entire neighborhood to enjoy while my mother was helplessly trying to calm him down. Her attempts were having no impact. This was, by far, the angriest I'd ever seen anybody. Then I looked over to see the most stomach-turning sight I'd ever seen. There was a long strip of burned black hole where the liner of the pool should have been. The hole was right above the water line. The pristine blue liner had been melted by fire. The hole was not small; it was seven feet of melted horror show. Our perfect pool we were so proud of was destroyed. Somebody had set fire to it, and we all knew who it was.

It didn't take Sherlock Holmes to put the pieces together. The evidence was staring straight at us from the bottom of the pool. As my mother was attempting to talk my father down from committing murder, I investigated the scene of the crime. Ten feet deep below the surface of the water lay a small Hibachi grill we had been using to cook hot dogs and hamburgers all summer. Now it was resting at the bottom of the pool like the god damned Titanic. Floating on top of the water was the saddest looking little hamburger patty I ever saw. It wasn't even fully cooked and it was just sitting in the middle of the pool. A small can of lighter fluid was laying on the cement above the violated pool liner. Looking at the can of lighter fluid, then at the floating burger, and finally at the tiny grill at the bottom of the pool; I was able to understand everything.

Jubby was trying to cook a burger and couldn't get the grill lit. He decided to use lighter fluid to solve the problem and ended up using way too much. The grill ignited into an uncontrollable blaze. Poor Jubby, in a full state of panic, picked up the Hibachi and held it in the pool water to extinguish the flame. He lost his grip and the entire apparatus fell into the water. The flaming lighter fluid splashed onto the liner during this debacle and melted it into the horrific sight we were now staring at in disbelief. The pool was ruined…destroyed. I remember thinking it was possible our flawed Cub Scout instructions in fire safety were somewhat to blame.

"I'm getting my shotgun."

Holy shit! That's what my father said. Oh my God! He was going to kill Jubby. This was bad. I felt sick.

"Billy, stop it!" My mother became assertive. This was a crisis, and she was going to have to prevent her husband from killing his youngest son.

She looked to me for help.

"Find your brother. Now."

I hopped on my bike and started riding. I was pretty sure I knew where Jubby would be. A few months before this, we had built a fort in the middle of some woods where we liked to trespass. It was our own personal safe spot and offered refuge when we felt like life was getting too crazy. We spent a lot of time there. It was hard to find and the perfect place to go if you were a kid who needed to run away from home for burning down the new family pool.

When I found him in the fort, he was terrified, like an animal caught in a trap.

"Dad's…(sob)…. going…(sob)…to…kill…me…(sob)."

"Probably."

I started crying too. I agreed, my father was going to kill him. First the car and now this, how could he not?

"What…(sob)…did…(sob)…he…(sob)…say…(sob)?"

"He said he was gonna get his shotgun."

"Oh GOD!"

We hugged each other for a while. Eventually I got him to calm down.

"What's in the backpack?" I asked.

"Snacks."

Good thinking. We shared some Animal Crackers and tried our best to steel ourselves and face the music. This time I would be by my brother's side. I felt too sorry for him. There was just no way I could let him face this by himself. With dread in our hearts, we peddled home side by side. I felt like puking; my brother must have felt like he was dying. I don't know how he gathered the courage to face my father, but he did. Before we knew it we were sheepishly entering the once beautiful pool yard that now felt like the worst place in the world.

When we got there, the sun was almost down. It was still a calm summer night, however, my father was anything but calm. He was sitting at the picnic table adjacent to the burned section of liner. The grill and the burger were still in the pool; nobody was going to tamper with the evidence until the accused could account for himself and his heinous crime. Jubby never looked so small as he did when my father stood up and looked down on him. With a shaking hand my father pointed at his brand-new pool. He was so angry that the words came out in a whisper.

"Why? Why did you do this?"

There was a long pause.

Jubby looked up from his shoes with tears streaming down his face.

"I was just trying to cook you a burger, Dad."

We all lost it. What do you say to that? My brother was trying to make up for having destroyed the car by cooking my father a hamburger. In the process of trying to get his father to forgive him, he ended up burning down the pool. What can anybody say to that? If you didn't laugh, you'd have to cry.

We did cry…all of us. That night wasn't easy. My father needed to get away from it all. At one point he disappeared and then reappeared with a shotgun in one hand and a bottle of Black Velvet in the other.

My mother was not happy.

"What are you doing?" she asked.

"I'm driving out to the woods to spend the night," he replied.

 She didn't argue. Instead, she commanded her sons to go with him.

"Boys, go with your father. He needs you."

"I want to stay with you," I cried to my mother.

"No. All three of you need to go with your father." She wasn't giving in.

We were all sobbing. Was he leaving us forever? Were my parents going to get a divorce? Nobody knew anything. I'm not sure if she thought our presence would prevent him from leaving the family forever. Maybe she was worried he'd pull a Hemingway and thought the presence of his boys would give him a reason to live. Either way, my brothers and I found ourselves camping out with our unstable father on a dirt road in the middle of nowhere. In retrospect, I think the decision to drive to the middle of the woods that night was a good choice. Most likely it worked better than anything to subdue his anger. In the morning, we woke up and the old man still seemed pissed, but at least he was ready to go home.

When we got back to the house, my parents hugged each other. He apologized and they resolved to find a way to repair the pool. My brothers and I were still semi-catatonic. We had been on a roller-coaster of emotions and it was hard to reconcile the events of the previous night. It was impossible to know how to feel. Were we being punished for having too much luck? Maybe this was God teaching us not to feel too proud, too lucky? I couldn't help but feel enormous sympathy for my brother throughout the ordeal. To me Jubby was always like that guy Job in the Bible; it was always one calamity after another. There had to be a reason for all that bad luck.

Eventually a phone call would be made to the guys who had installed the pool. There was a collective sigh of relief when we found out that repairing a burned pool liner is not terribly hard. In the matter of a few hours the pool guys showed up and put a patch on the damaged spot. It was fixed and looked fine. It wasn't as nice as it once was, but it was fine.

Amazingly, during this entire terrible incident my father never actually asked the question "Why can't we have anything nice?" I'd like to think that in the middle of the night while camping out with his three sons in his Chevy van, my dad reflected on a lot of things. He came to terms with the car and the pool being destroyed. They were only material things and each would be fixed. I like to imagine that he looked at his sons sleeping in the family van and thought about his wife at home. He must have had a moment in which he saw that, despite the destruction of so many of his possessions, he had *something nice* all along. Everything was going to be okay.

$$11$$

The Bicycle Story

To an eleven-year-old kid growing up in a small town, a bike is more than just a bike. Sure, it's what he depends on to get him from here to there. But it's more than that. It's his personality. It's social status. It's freedom. It's fun. It's everything. The most meaningful journey a kid takes on his bike isn't even to a destination. Rather, it's a symbolic mode of transportation propelling a kid toward inevitable adulthood. A kid's bicycle can be his best companion. For every cowboy who loved his horse, there is a kid who would be faithfully loyal to the metal steed that has two wheels, a seat, and handlebars. In the fall of my sixth-grade year, I loved few things more than I loved my bike. However, on one fateful day the bicycle I adored, nearly as much as I loved my own mother, would act as an instrument that threatened not only my own existence, but the existence of my future children.

Jubby and I had the same exact bikes. They were given to us on our birthday. It was probably one of the best birthdays ever. I still remember coming out to the yard and seeing them for the first time. Two bikes were standing side by side propped up by kickstands. They were the same. They looked as identical as Jubby and I were fraternal. You get used to having a lot of the same things when you're a twin. Most of the time it kind of sucks. Matching toys, matching radios, matching beds, matching sneakers, matching socks, matching underwear, matching everything. Getting a bunch of the same stuff is just part of the deal. Most of the time we didn't like it, but having matching bicycles was cool to us.

The bicycles were fire engine red. They weren't like our friends' BMX bikes. Those were sporty and would prove to be better for jumping and skidding around. Ours weren't like that at all. For some reason, our parents bought us bikes that were completely different and unique from everyone else's. They were banana seat bikes that resembled choppers. The handlebars came directly out of a knob in the center and extended out and then up and then out again. You rode with your arms reaching straight out from your shoulders while your butt sat comfortably on the long black banana shaped seat which had a metal loop handle on the back of it. At first, I felt a little self-conscious that our bikes weren't like our friends', but I soon grew to think it was cool. I liked the fact that my bike was different. It set Jubby and me apart from everyone else and let everyone know that he and I were together; here come *The Heaney Twins*. If only I could have known how much pain I would suffer from the best present I'd ever gotten!

I have established, already, that my twin brother was a destructive kid. Again, he didn't mean to break stuff. He was just rambunctious and impetuous. Material possessions don't stand a chance with that combination. For me, the biggest problems would occur when Jubby broke his bicycle, which happened often. Whenever this took place, I would be expected to be a good sibling and share *my* precious bike with him. I didn't like doing this but most of the time I would end up giving in and sharing. It wasn't fair but being a kid is all about dealing with stuff that isn't fair. "Just be careful with it," I would nervously say. Then I'd watch as he would treat my bike in ways that made me cringe.

It was a Sunday evening when it happened. It was autumn and we had school the next day. Rather than do our homework, my friends and I decided to ride around town. Jubby had been "working" on his bike all day, but it was broken and would need professional care to be resurrected. He was beyond frustrated. Everyone else had a bike while his was completely un-ridable.

"You need to share your bike with me."

"No."

I didn't want to. I took care of my bike, and it bothered me that I would have to pay the consequences because he was rough with his his.

"Come on," he threatened.

His tone was menacing, and I immediately realized I'd have to relent, otherwise, there would be hell to pay. Jubby and I could be best friends, but we could also be worst enemies. He was bigger than me and stronger than me. Most of the time I didn't want to face his wrath, which would almost always end in me being held down, shoulders pinned to the ground by his knees while he spit in my face. This was almost a daily occurrence and I lived in constant fear of it. Realizing that if I didn't share my bike with him during this outing with friends, I'd be suffering some kind of public humiliation at the hands of an enraged twin who, having run out of things to break, might just break me.

"Okay." I gave in. I didn't want to, but I also didn't want to get my ass kicked for the thousandth time.

And so, a handful of us began riding around town as we always did. Outside of Jubby sitting shotgun behind me, nothing was out of the ordinary. I had no premonition of what was about to happen. We rode down one of our favorite streets. We passed the Protestant Cemetery in a tight pack. I peddled along while Jubby sat behind me on the banana seat. Then, for some reason, he decided to hop off while we were still going. I kept peddling.

"STOP!!"

He yelled it. He wanted to get back on.

I must have become frustrated with the constant stopping and starting that went along with sharing the bike that evening. I decided to ignore his command. I kept peddling with him running after me.

"STOP!" He yelled again.

I didn't. I was defying him, and he was growing noticeably angrier as he continued to yell for me to halt. There was definite threat in his tone. He said "stop" but what he really meant was "I'm going to kick your ass when I get ahold of you." It was a real Catch-22. Stop and get pummeled in front of your friends immediately or keep riding until he catches up with you later and then get pummeled even worse. I kept riding until I came to the bridge that crossed the river. Out of fear of consequences, I decided it would be wisest to wait for my brother and let him get back on.

It wasn't a heavily trafficked road. I was straddling my bike while my friends caught up to me. Then came Jubby. He was running. He was out of breath. He was enraged. I was going to be in deep shit, and I knew it. I figured I'd get slapped around a little bit and would have to relinquish my bicycle and walk back home. Oh, how I wish that would have been the case.

The bridge was in front of me. A crummy looking trailer down a muddy driveway was on my left. There really was no way to escape my brother who was coming at me with violence in his heart.

"I TOLD YOU TO STOP!!"

I'm sure he had a lot of pent-up frustration from his own bike being broken, and he needed to let it out in some way. He grabbed the handle on the back of the banana seat while I was straddling the bar with both feet on the ground. With freakish strength that went well beyond what an eleven-year-old should have, Jubby yanked the bike forward and then pulled it backward as hard as he could. Basic physics took over. My scrawny ninety-pound body flew backwards and then suddenly reversed course to fly forward at breakneck speed.

It's hard to explain how hard my little groin slammed against the sharp middle portion of the handlebars. It was a direct hit though and there was a kind of splat sound that accompanied the impact. It might have been like the kind of sound a pancake would make if you threw it against a wall as hard as you could.

THWAP!

My crotch suffered a violent collision, immediately came to a halt, and then kind of balanced on the handlebars. At the same time, the upper part of my body continued forward until it was jerked backward. Meanwhile the most sensitive part of my body remained smashed against the sharp metallic portion of the handlebars. It all happened so fast that it was hard to process what had just happened. The stinging sensation was immediate. So was the knowledge that something was terribly, terribly wrong. I jumped off the bike as fast as I could in a state of panic.

"OH SHIT, OH SHIT, OH SHIT, OH SHIT, OH SHIT, OH SHIT, OH SHIT!!!

The pain was unbearable. Oh! My! God! Suddenly I was not in control of what I was saying or doing. I was jumping up and down while holding my privates. My friends and my brother were looking at me in complete amazement. They laughed at first but now they realized something was very, very wrong with me. I wasn't even able to yell or scream anymore. I needed to look; I needed to see what had happened inside my pants.

"Oh shit. Oh my God. Oh shit."

I had to look. I didn't want to. It was terrifying. Whatever I was feeling inside my pants wasn't going to be good to look at. Oh, my God! What was I going to do? The pain was so extreme that I couldn't breathe. I was hyperventilating. I was in a panic. The world was spinning around me. I didn't even know my name at this point. I pulled my jeans away from myself and looked down into my underpants to see what reminded me of a bowl of Campbell's tomato soup. I couldn't see anything except a tighty-whitey filled pool of my own blood. Somewhere, swimming around in all that blood, might be the freshly severed penis of an eleven-year-old boy.

"AHHHHHHHHHHHHHHHHHHHHHHHHHHHHH!!!!!!"

I screamed louder than any little boy has ever screamed…ever. There is no doubt in my mind that I set a world record for volume in that moment. My friends were frozen. They had no idea what I'd just seen.

"MY DICK! MY DICK! MY DICK! AHHHHHHHHH!"

"What? What is it? What's Wrong?"

My friends were trying to calm me down, but they didn't know. What I had seen was beyond my worst nightmare. There was no way for my friends to comprehend the dilemma I'd just found myself in. None of them had ever looked down into their underpants to find old Moby Dick lost in the Red Sea.

"MY DICK IS GONE! MY DICK IS GONE!!"

"What!?"

I was losing it and couldn't control myself. The world was spinning around me and my friends had no idea what to do.

All the sudden a stocky woman in a bathrobe was grabbing me by the shoulders. Apparently, she had been in her trailer taking a shower when she heard my screaming and assumed somebody was being violently murdered. Little did she know that this was way worse than any murder. This was child castration by way of bicycle. Then the woman was shooing my friends away and guiding me into the trailer. I was done screaming and had become catatonic. Every part of me was shaking. I was like a soldier suffering from paralyzing shellshock. My life, as I knew it, was over. The blood that was seeping through my underwear and staining my jeans was an indicator that life might never be the same again. The reality of it was too much to handle. I couldn't get the sight of the "tomato soup" in my undies out of my head.

The woman sat me at the circular table in her little kitchenette. I heard her voice as if it was coming from a great distance. How does getting your penis cut off damage your hearing? I looked through my tears and saw her lips moving.

"What's your phone number?"

"Huh."

"I need to call your parents. What's your phone number?"

I have no recollection of telling her the digits to reach my parents, but I guess I must have figured it out. I sat in the trailer shaking uncontrollably until my mother came in to find me. From the pain I was feeling and the sight of blood overflowing in my underpants, there was reason to believe I no longer possessed a penis. My mother knocked on the trailer door and came in. One look at her and I lost it again.

I cried out, "Mom, I'm hurt. I'm hurt so bad. Mommy. I'm scared. I'm scared. I'm really hurt."

"I know. Let's go home."

She drove me home and we went immediately to the bathroom. My father and my older brother looked stricken and sick. They were assuming the worst. Jubby "The Castrating Wonder" was nowhere to be found. Destroying the pool liner was one thing. Cutting off your brother's penis was something on an entire other level. My mother had me stand in the bathtub. She was trying to calm my nerves. This wasn't going to be easy.

She asked me to take my pants off.

"I can't. I don't want to."

"You have to."

It went on like that for a long time. I couldn't bear to look. The horror was awful. The pain was already unbearable, and it wasn't subsiding but seeing my own severed penis might actually kill me. My mother, God bless her, was remarkably calm. Eventually she coaxed me into peeling off my blood-soaked jeans.

Then came the hardest part. When I got dressed at the beginning of the day, my underpants had been pure white, the classic little kid tighty-whiteys. Now, it was as if somebody had poured an entire bottle of Hunt's Ketchup all over them. My hands were shaking uncontrollably as I peeled the undergarment from my hips and down to my knees. I closed my eyes. I couldn't bear to look. The stinging pain was terrible, but I couldn't look. And then…

"It's going to be okay." That was what my mother said after all was revealed.

"What?"

I opened my eyes and looked down. It wasn't pretty…not by a long shot. In fact, it was *pretty* awful. I was looking at something resembling a hot dog that had been left on the grill too long and was now split open and charred black, but I still had a penis that was attached to the rest of my body. It wasn't cut off. It was terribly lacerated and bruised but it wasn't lost and gone forever.

"Is he okay?" I heard my father call from the other side of the bathroom door.

"He's going to be alright…I think."

I wasn't sure. I certainly wasn't an expert on the recovery power of the human penis. All I knew at the time was that I was in a lot of pain and that getting kicked in the balls was nothing compared to this. Also, my downstairs had been mangled pretty good. It looked like it had gone twelve rounds with the heavyweight champ and taken the worst beating of its life.

Jubby finally showed up. He was crying and pleading for forgiveness. Of course, my father lost it on him.

"You broke your brother's penis! You should be ashamed of yourself!"

He was. I know he felt bad. There was no getting around it. He had, in fact, broken his twin brother's penis and he'd have to forgive himself for it. It's not easy to live something like that down. I wasn't exactly happy with him, and it would take a while, but eventually I forgave him. He hadn't intended for this to happen.

Good fortune often goes along with bad. One silver lining that came out of this calamity was that I couldn't go to school for an entire week. It was impossible to wear clothing below the belt line; it just wasn't going to happen. I spent the week on the couch dressed only in a bathrobe. I had to tent up the middle section of the robe with a wooden spoon as I lay there trying to ignore the stinging sensation I feared would never go away. Every time I looked at my damaged goods, I hoped to see improvement. The worst was that I couldn't even pee for a few days, the plumbing didn't want to work. As the week went by things started to improve. Thank God. Old "Frankenpenis" began to heal. The lacerations wouldn't need stitches. Amazingly, my parents chose not to take their son with a flayed penis to the doctor. They were probably baffled as to how to make the appointment.

"Ahhh, yeah I'd like to make an appointment for my son to see the doctor."

"Sure. What seems to be the problem?"

"Uhhh…so…well…his brother…ummm…let's just say we're worried we might not get future grandkids someday."

Soon I was able to wear regular clothes and didn't have to walk around the house hunched over in a bathrobe, trying to avoid the friction of any article of clothing against my injury. By the end of the week, I could put on some loose-fitting boxers and some sweatpants. It was relieving to find that I healed quickly. Everything eventually started working again. Whew!

Amazingly, my friends kept it a secret. They knew what happened and the pity they felt must have prevented them from talking about it at school. When I returned to the sixth-grade classroom, my classmates just knew that I had had a bike accident and that they shouldn't ask me about it. They didn't. And life eventually returned to normal. As the saying goes, time heals all wounds… even lacerations on a kid's private parts.

A few weeks after the accident I decided that I wanted to ride my bike again. I couldn't stop thinking about my bicycle, the bicycle that had been given to me for my birthday. It had been my favorite possession. It had been my freedom. It had given me so much joy. It had taken me everywhere. But something was different. Now it had been an instrument that had caused me so much pain. It held a menace it didn't have before and so did life. The accident had made me feel vulnerable and fearful, I felt raw. My physical wounds had healed, but I was a nervous wreck. I didn't tell anybody, but I was feeling a fear that I couldn't fully comprehend. I wasn't old enough to understand the idea of existential dread, but that's what it was. The thought that something bad could happen to me at any moment was consuming my thoughts. I was at a crossroads.

The bike had been stored in the garage unridden for a few weeks. It stood there beckoning me. It was telling me something. It wanted me to ride it. I looked at it for a long time, unsure if I should get back on it. I felt scared to ride it again, but I also felt like I'd hate myself if I didn't. This thinking went on for a long time.

Then, in a moment of clarity, I made a decision. It might seem like a small decision, but it wasn't. For me it was enormous. This was a decision where one defines who they are and the kind of person they're going to be for the rest of their lives. It turns out that all the cliches are true. Life can knock you down. Sometimes it kicks you in the teeth. You get curveballs thrown at you when you least expect them. Sometimes life even threatens to rip your manhood right off your little eleven-year-old bones. Bad things, through no fault of your own, are going to happen. It's a certainty. The true test is being able to pick yourself up, brush yourself off, and keep going. I know these are the lessons from just about every sports movie ever made, but I don't care. They happen to be true. I'm certainly not the first to echo these sentiments and I won't be the last. I had earned something through my pain. My painful experience had given me a gift, the gift of perspective.

I didn't know it then, but this accident would teach me one of the most important lessons of my life. If I'd had a crystal ball to see into the future, I would have discovered that almost losing my penis in a freak accident was one of the best things that ever happened to me. It didn't kill me, and I don't think it made me tougher. It made me appreciate the importance of resilience. Bad things happen; scary things happen. It's okay. Keep going. I'm proud to say that, after all I'd been through, I got back on my bike, and I started riding again.

12

The Semi-Stigmatic Boy

"There is a thin line that separates the difference between comedy and tragedy. Tragedy is when I fall down the stairs. Comedy is when you fall down the stairs."

A literature professor in college told me that and I always remembered it because it applied to my life in ways my professor couldn't have known. It's amazing how much time you spend in school and how few things you remember. We tend to remember things because they are funny, they are painful, or they are out of the ordinary. Most days tend to be a facsimile of the day that came before it and that tends to mess with our memories later. The memorable days almost always involve either laughter or tears.

School assemblies made me laugh. There was always something so funny about being in an entire crowd full of eager kids waiting to see something that would invariably be terribly disappointing. The agenda for a school assembly is always transparent. Don't smoke. Don't do drugs. Stranger Danger!! Show kindness. Don't be a bully. Use a condom. The common motif is for kids not to partake in some kind of activity that is on the PTO's radar. Often, assemblies show how out of touch schools can be with kids. This is the best part of assemblies and what makes them so funny. The school is almost always trying hard to catch up to what's "hip" with the kids and falling short of the mark. You can imagine a principal along with other school officials getting together at a meeting and discussing how to reach "kids these days."

"What are we going to do about all these kids smoking cigarettes?"

"I have an idea. You know how the kids really love that hippity-hop rap music these days? Maybe we should have somebody come in and do a rap that tells them that smoking cigarettes will ruin their lives."

"Great idea. The kids will love it!"

Flash to an audience full of kids not having a clue what to make of "DJ Just Say No" laying down a fat beat about not *getting ciggy with it*.

When I was in elementary school there were a couple assemblies that stood out from the rest. One assembly offered a pathetic attempt to fix one of the worst issues in society at the time, *the excessive noise during lunch in the cafeteria.* Apparently, the lunch ladies in school threw a terrible conniption fit in front of the principal. Something had to be done to get the little brats to shut the hell up and just eat their mystery meat. What was the administration going to do about it? There would be only one way to properly address the issue: *Assembly.*

Imagine hundreds of elementary school kids sitting in an auditorium. I was smack dabbed in the middle of the audience. We had been told for weeks that the school had ordered something that was going to revolutionize our school. We were told it would change our lives forever and it would be the greatest thing we would ever see. The principal went around saying, "You just wait until *it* comes." We all talked about what the "it" must be. Was the school going to install a new swimming pool? Were we going to get new athletic equipment? Was somebody famous coming to our school? Nobody knew anything, not even the teachers.

The day of the much-anticipated assembly arrived. There was going to be some kind of "big reveal." The school principal bounded out to the stage to quiet us down. The audience was full of excitement because the mystery had caused somewhat of a stir. What was this thing that was going to "change our lives forever?" We settled down to listen. The build-up had been effective. For once, we were assembled and eager. A few weeks of debate, discussion and speculation had made even the most cynical kid a little curious.

"Today is the day we've been waiting for!" the principal announced.

As soon as this was said, the green auditorium curtain was pulled back to reveal a shrouded ten-foot-tall object in the middle of the stage. You could tell that the administration had put a little bit of thought into the production value of the event, but just a little bit. The initial reaction was silence. What were we supposed to think? There was a very tall object on the stage that was covered with a black tarp. It didn't move; it just sat there like the monolith in *2001: A Space Odyssey.* Nobody knew what it could be. The shroud was covering it completely and the only thing you could tell was that it was tall and thin. Other than that, nothing.

After a few seconds of bafflement, the crowd fell into line and offered the expected participation. Even this low-grade version of a Showcase Showdown reveal was enough to rile us up. Chanting began.

"Take it off! Take it off! Take it off!"

The principal, getting off on this excitement, became like a friggin' magician. The guy was swirling around the mystery object while making all sorts of weird gesticulations with his hands; he was in his glory. It was surreal, like watching some bizarro version of a coked-up *Price is Right* model fawning all over the unknown item that had yet to be revealed. His act was making an impact. We weren't laughing. Mob mentality had gotten ahold of us, and we were in its grip. There was only one thing that mattered at that moment.

"Take it off! Take it off!" The chant built to its crescendo until the principal put his finger to his lips. We shut up. This would be "the big reveal." It was the moment we had been waiting for. Someday we would tell our grandkids about this. The entire audience leaned in with mouths agape. Silence.

Then he pulled the shroud revealing something not a single person expected. It was a god damned traffic light.

What the hell!? A traffic light!?

We were dumbfounded. Nobody could talk.

"It's a State-of-the-Art Sound Sensitive Cafeteria Monitor!" the principal yelled.

"Booooo!"

The crowd erupted with a cacophony of disappointed jeers.

"People, people, settle down. Let me show you how it works."

Once we were calm, he proceeded to demonstrate how the machine was supposed to work by asking us to make levels of noise. It didn't take a genius to see the basic plan. A green light was an indicator of acceptable noise level, yellow was meant to put us on alert as we were getting a bit too rowdy, and red was telling us that we were godless heathens who needed to shut the hell up immediately.

What a gyp! We were duped. That's an assembly for you. Just another example of a lame-brained way to get an agenda across. The traffic light eventually made its way to the cafeteria only to make things far worse. Kids couldn't resist coordinating well-timed loud noises to keep the light toggling between yellow and red to drive the cafeteria monitors bonkers. Those poor ladies had it bad enough having to wear hair nets all day, now this.

For the remainder of my school years, this object of disappointment was a monument of derision. It just sat in the middle of the cafeteria being mocked day in and day out. Not a single kid ever respected it. The lights would just toggle between green and red for a few years while nobody paid attention. Eventually it would be unplugged and sit there gathering dust. What a waste. But it had taught us a valuable lesson: Don't get your hopes up, especially when something seems like it's being sold to you. Experience is the best teacher of all, and this one would give us a healthy skepticism about the agenda of authority. It was another unintended silver lining.

There were many other assemblies. Most were boring and uneventful, but they all had one thing in common, each served some kind of agenda and we had become perpetual cynics. However, there was *one* assembly that proved memorable and had the power to override our disgruntled little hearts. This assembly was right up front and didn't beat around any bush because it was concerned with an announcement of the installation of a *new playground*. Students deserved to be excited at this assembly. A new playground is no joke. When you're a kid, your imagination goes wild about what a new playground will have.

The old one was a deathtrap built in the 1930s when people were constructing playgrounds designed to permanently maim or kill children brave enough to play on them. The Great Depression must have inspired people to thin out the herd by creating structures that offered a high risk of serious injury or death. The slides were mile-high towers that took ninja-like skill to scale the way-too-steep stairs. You'd get vertigo if you were brave enough to get to the top, and then you had to go down a slide that was like a ninety degree drop to the ground. Then there were the other major rides. There was the merry-go-round that would make a kid vomit after his friends pushed the thing to maximum speed for five straight minutes. How was that thing safe? The old school teeter-totters would just prove to incite practical jokes as kids would figure out how to jump off the teeter at the right moment and cause the totter to slam to the ground and suffer a broken tailbone. Everywhere you looked kids were walking around looking like they suffered from a serious case of scoliosis. Something had to change; kids' lives were in danger, and something had to be done.

Again, the PTO came to the rescue. Everyone agreed that the old playground was going to kill somebody. It was unanimous, so they decided to round up the funds to get something called a "Creative Playground." Apparently the "Creative Playground" was all the rage in the 80s. Every school in America started revamping the old metal death playgrounds into elaborate wonderlands. These new structures looked more like castles than anything else. They were almost completely made of wood. Multiple slides and swings were built in and around the structure. There were fancy monkey bars and multiple balancing beams shooting off in all directions. In one spot, discarded farm equipment was used to create a tractor-tire obstacle course. There were bridges and towers and hidden rooms and all sorts of things that gave it the impression of a medieval fortress. It was awesome! The construction happened rather quickly. SHAZAM! Within two weeks, the old playground was demolished and a new one rose from its ashes.

However, at first it was off limits. The playground had been taped off to let us know it wasn't to be played on just yet. There had to be *another* assembly to go over the new playground rules. Assemblies are like that; one leads to another. It's not hard to imagine a dystopian world where eventually life is nothing but a constant assembly. The authority figures schedule an assembly to discuss having another assembly. Nonetheless, our patience would be tested, we were eager. The new playground was a reality, and we couldn't wait to use it.

Once again, the principal was in front of an entire school of elementary children. There was no magic act or cheesy reveal of anything this time. He had learned his lesson. This time he was all business. Regardless, this would still be an assembly with an agenda. Mostly, it was an attempt to lay down the law and persuade child heathens to respect this new construction that we "should feel so lucky to have." After twenty minutes of rules and regulations, the principal got around to the most important point. He told us that the playground would not be officially opened until one thing happened. All of us needed to use "our ticket."

"Ticket?"

We all looked at each other. What did he mean by "ticket?"

Then we found out. Like clockwork, our teachers came around handing out a piece of sandpaper. Every single student sitting in the assembly got one. We could see what was happening. We weren't stupid. At least, we weren't that stupid.

"You're going to use your ticket to sand down the new playground. It's full of slivers and it's up to you guys to get out there and make this playground safe for generations of kids to use. Now go out and get at that playground!"

He yelled it like he expected us to jump out of our seats with sandpaper in our hands and violently stampede toward the playground yelling and screaming like we were soldiers charging the beach at Normandy. His excitement didn't really carry over to us. In fact, we just sat looking at the sandpaper. More propaganda. This assembly was designed to turn us into child laborers. I'm sure they thought it would give us pride and some feeling of ownership over our new playground and, to a certain extent, they were right. At the time we just felt like we were being duped into doing a job the guys who built the thing should have done.

After a full day of sanding playground wood, the yellow police tape was taken down and we were finally allowed to romp all over this beautiful new construction. It was an immediate hit and we loved it. We also discovered why it was called a "Creative Playground." Kids could use their imaginations to invent all sorts of activities on their own. It was a shenanigan producing machine. Some of the games we played were standard. There were the tried-and-true standbys: Hide and seek and freeze tag. There were role-playing games in which we acted like soldiers and ninjas and killer robots. Then there were other games that would be more antagonizing.

These are the games that kids love the most, where the playground becomes like the setting of *Lord of the Flies*. The activity of the playground morphs into a microcosm of society. Games aren't just games, they're powerplays. Survival of the fittest and natural selection would be tested every day during recess. One game we liked to play, that fit into this category, didn't actually have a name. We would just conspire to get under the skin of our peers by stealing something from them and then hiding it somewhere in the labyrinthian structure of the new playground. Then we would take sadistic pleasure watching our victim look all over the playground for the stolen item. They would beg for clues that would never be offered. Little kids can be such punks.

Despite the endless amounts of pleasure I enjoyed from our new playground, there was one moment that proved not to be fun at all. In fact, it would be the opposite of fun. During one playtime, I was being a little turd and had stolen a friend's hat with the intention of hiding it and tormenting him. I found myself shimmying up a twenty-foot triangular wooden structure to place the snatched object at the top point. I thought it would be funny for everyone to see his hat at the highest point of the wooden pyramid while my friend would have to climb up to get it with everyone watching. How clever I thought I was. After successfully completing the task of putting the hat at the top of the structure, I slid down the wooden beam diagonally angled toward the ground. While my arms and legs hugged the wooden descent, my belly did most of the sliding. Halfway down I heard a "Craaaack!" and simultaneously felt a sharp stabbing pain in my mid-section.

Quickly hitting the ground, I lifted my shirt to find that, whilst sliding down, I had snagged a sliver that some kid obviously failed to smooth out with his sandpaper ticket. Upon further inspection, I realized I was in trouble. This wasn't just any sliver; this thing was a jagged chuck of treated lumber. A goddamned two by four was sticking out of me. I was impaled by what looked like an angry piece of driftwood. To make matters worse, it had found a terrible resting place: My bellybutton. It was a direct hit, too, like an arrow sticking straight out of a bullseye.

I headed over to my teacher, lifting my shirt and pointing out that I'd just been skewered. "Shish kaboy." Thankfully, there was no blood and the pain was only mild. I was calm, all things considered.

"Ummmm. Can I go to the nurse?"

"Oooooh. Yeah. Go now!"

The next thing I knew I was in the nurse's office. She was douching my bellybutton with hydrogen peroxide as I'm standing with a good chunk of playground sticking out of my inny. Then she starts trying to pull it out.

"Tough little bugger, isn't it?"

She begins tugging harder, but the thing doesn't budge. The only thing happening is that my entire little body is being pulled toward her. Out of frustration, she makes me hang on to the frame of the door as she's yanking and yanking on this thing, but it isn't going anywhere. Now she is beyond frustrated and decides to take another course of action.

"Hold on. I've got an idea."

Suddenly, she is on the phone.

"Ray. Can you come up here with your toolbox?"

In seconds, Ray the janitor is in the room.

"Got some pliers?"

"Yep."

The tool is pulled from its box, and I'm told to lay down on the nurse's bed. The nurse and the school janitor are hovering over me like two surgeons. They tell me just to look up at the ceiling as Ray latches on to this new appendage that is protruding from the spot that used to hook me to my mother while in-utero. I feel Ray start tugging. Amazingly my whole body starts being lifted from the mid-section as the pliers are attempting to pull the wood from me. I'm pulled up about two feet from the bed and then let back down. Nothing. The wood was still there.

"Let's try this. You push down on his chest while I use the pliers to pull again."

The nurse straddles over me as I continue to look up at the ceiling. I'm not in pain, but I am concerned I might have to go through life with a four-inch splinter jutting out of my belly.

Ray begins pulling again.

"Come on you little piece of crap!"

I hope he is talking to the splinter and not me.

POP! Thank God. It came out. We all breathe a sigh of relief and ten minutes later I am back on the playground.

It turned out this event was a dress-rehearsal for something that would happen next. In the great cause and effect chain of life, it would foreshadow a nightmare right around the corner. Apparently, it was "puncture wound season" and nobody told me. About a week after the splinter had entered my abdomen, I found myself playing at a friend's house. I didn't know it yet, but this would end up being one of those memorable days. You don't forget the kind of pain I felt that day.

We were playing tag. Tag wasn't just a game with us. It was a blood-sport and we took it seriously. Often it felt like a game of life and death. We would chase and be chased with an intensity that made you forget everything else in life. We would become maniacs avoiding the dreaded label of being "it." To be "it" was akin to being a loser. This day, my friend James was "it." We were all running around in my friend's side yard like little savages. James' father, Mark, was somewhat of a carpenter and had all sorts of wood laying all around the yard. It looked a little bit like a construction zone, but it didn't matter to us. Tag could be played anywhere, and we were never terribly concerned with safety.

The day was hot. I remember breathing heavily and running as James was chasing me. I zigged and zagged and ran like crazy. He was fast and right on my heels as I tried to evade him. I was running like the wind but then something was wrong, my stride was off. My right foot was stepping down an inch higher than it had been just a second before. I stopped as James caught up and tagged me.

"You're it!"

"Hold on."

"What's wrong?"

Looking down at my foot, I saw a strange sight. There was a block of wood stuck to the bottom of my sneaker.

"Huh. That's funny."

I reached down and tried to pull it away from my foot. I figured it must have glue or gum or something that was sticking it to the bottom of my sneaker. I pulled but it didn't budge. Then I felt the pain. It was a sharp pain like fire in the middle of my foot. At the very moment that I felt the pain I saw the reason for it, and the explanation for the piece of wood being stuck to my foot. A sharp, rusty spike was sticking out of the top of my Nike. Blood was dripping from the point of it. My foot had been fully impaled from both sides by a sharp nail sticking out of the block of wood.

I fell to the ground.

"Ahhhhhhhhhhhhhhh!!"

The horror. God help me. I couldn't believe what was happening. There was a bloody spike sticking out of my shoe. Now, the block of wood and spike were part of me. To say that I freaked out would be an understatement. I was having convulsions like I was possessed by demons. Instant hyper-ventilation. I could only think to keep blurting out the same words over and over.

"MY FOOT! MY FOOT! MY FOOT!"

It had only been a year prior that I was yelling a similar phrase regarding a decidedly more sensitive body part.

Then James's mom was above me. She took one look at my foot and erupted.

"GOD DAMN IT MARK! I TOLD HIM NOT TO LEAVE THIS WOOD LAYING AROUND!"

The woman picked up my foot and put it in a bear hug. I remember just looking up at her back as she had my ankle in between her side and the crook of her left arm. She took her right hand and grabbed the block that was nailed to my foot. She wrenched the piece of wood away from my body with all the strength she had. The woman wasn't messing around.

"AHHHHHHHHHHH!"

The pain was intense, like electricity shooting from the top of my foot all the way through and out the arch. It took me a while to calm down. In the meantime, a phone call was made to my mother. Within a few minutes she showed up and I found myself headed to the doctor's office. The car ride was full of tears and worry. I had a strong sense of déjà vu.

"What's the doctor going to do?"

"He's probably just going to give you a tetanus shot."

"What's that?"

"It'll prevent you from getting lockjaw."

"What's that?"

"It's when you're jaw clamps shut forever because you have an infection in your body from a rusty nail."

Holy Jeez. The things you find out when you're a kid! The tetanus shot seemed like something I wouldn't want to turn down.

We got to the doctor's office, and I found myself lying on his bed. The double-impaled shoe was being examined with great curiosity. My mother had also brought the rusty nail and block of wood for examination. It was like show and tell.

"Well, I'll be. They really got you, didn't they?" the doctor said.

"Looks like we'll have to give the boy a tetanus shot. Then we're going to have to clean out the wound."

The nurse brought in the supplies. The tetanus shot was fine, just a shot in the arm. I'd had lots of those. Then I watched as the doctor began fixing a long needle to a syringe that had a clear liquid inside it.

"There's a lot of rust and dirt in the wound and it's likely to cause infection. You probably don't want to lose your leg or die, I'm assuming?"

I just nod.

"I'm going to use this needle to clean out the injury and prevent that from happening. I'm sorry, but it's going to be a little painful."

The doctor told me to lay on my belly. He told my mother to hold me down. And then he approached my wounded foot with the needle.

Now would be a good time to tell you something about my doctor. He had been my physician throughout my childhood, and he was a very nice man. I liked him immensely, however, there was something I didn't like about him. The poor guy was afflicted with Parkinson's Disease. When he looked in your ears and up your nose you couldn't help but be worried about the uncontrolled vibrations of the man's hands as he shook uncontrollably while inserting instruments inside your head. I remember being worried that he might accidentally break my eardrum while investigating an ear infection. During a physical, when he had you "drop your drawers" and "turn your head and cough" while checking your private parts for a hernia, the accompanying tremors were particularly unsettling. Now, this very shaky-handed doctor was going to be inserting a needle into the puncture wound at the bottom of my foot.

The needle entered the arch and I immediately hit the roof. I screamed so loud that I'm sure everyone in the waiting room thought I was dying. I'd felt a lot of painful things in my young life, but this was head-and-shoulders above the most excruciating things I had ever experienced. This was insanity-inducing. It wasn't pain; I'd felt pain. Pain was tolerable. This was true agony. I continued to scream and scream.

"I CAN'T TAKE IT. I CAN'T TAKE IT. PLEASE STOP. PLEASE STOP. PLEAAASE!"

My mother held me down as the man moved the needle into the middle of my foot to clean out all the gunk that was threatening my life and limb. It went on forever. Unphased by my screams, he kept rotating the needle around. I wasn't convinced that lockjaw would be worse than this. Hell, I wasn't convinced that losing my entire leg was worse than this. He scraped that needle around and around until I felt like I was going to faint, then he pulled it out.

"Let him catch his breath," the doctor said.

My mother soothed me and tried to get me to calm down. About a minute went by.

"Okay, we've got to clean the puncture on the top of the foot now."

"NOOOOOOOOOO!"

My pleading did no good. He spent the next five minutes inserting the needle into the other hole as I went in and out of consciousness.

I read a lot as a kid. I had a fascinating book that scared the crap out of me. It was a book about strange, unexplained phenomena in the world. I was enraptured with tales of ghost stories and hauntings. There were illustrations of the Loch Ness Monster and Bigfoot. It also had stories about black holes and other celestial mysteries. I was super freaked out about the phenomenon of spontaneous human combustion.

But the stories that stuck with me more than anything involved *stigmata*. What was stigmata? The book contained graphic pictures of people's wounded hands and feet. They looked like they had been punctured. Under the picture was a caption that said stigmata was a phenomenon where people were inexplicably struck with the wounds of Christ. After reading about this, I spent days imagining that it might happen to me. The book said that only the purest of people would be struck with stigmata. Considering that, I figured I wasn't in too much danger, but what did I know? I was only eleven.

After my season of impalement, I would consider myself a semi-stigmatic boy. Within the space of a couple weeks, I had been pierced in my abdomen like Christ being pierced by a Roman soldier. More significantly, my foot had been impaled by a spike in a similar fashion to poor old Jesus's a couple thousand years ago. Did this count as stigmata, I would wonder. Hey, two out of five ain't bad.

Maybe there's not really a thin line between comedy and tragedy. Maybe they're the same thing and we must learn to laugh through the pain.

13

Therapy Pets

My family always had pets when I was growing up, mostly one dog and one cat. We had a prim and proper cat named Priscilla who minded her own business. She was a lot like me. We both liked to stay away from the insanity as much as we could.

We also had a mutt named Bosworth that we affectionately called "Boz." Boz had no real discernable breed. He was black and white and showed little sign of intelligence. He had two skills in life, barking all the time and perpetually pissing off my old man. Boz's presence in our lives was all Jubby's fault. One summer day, when we were in elementary school, Jubby confronted my parents cradling a small puppy. The owner of the local diner, looking to unload a litter, flagged little Jubby down and made the transaction. Jubby was an easy target, and the dog was free. Everybody wins…sort of.

The dog and cat lived with us for close to twenty years. Out of everybody in the family, these two brought my mother the most joy. She had grown up on a farm and, as a science teacher, was also a real-life Dr. Doolittle. Some people just have a magic touch with animals. My mother was one of those people. It really seemed like she had the ability to speak with animals. It was amazing. Stray dogs and cats would follow her home. She'd spend hundreds of dollars feeding birds in the neighborhood. When we had a rodent in the house, she'd even insist on using traps that wouldn't kill them.

Her love of animals led to a living situation that was truly bizarre. It was something I loathed from the very beginning, and it only got worse with time. With the best of intentions, bad things can happen. In this case the best of intentions resulted in violence, murder, and severe bodily harm.

There were a lot of funny things about my parents. One thing that was always amusing was my father's attempts to give gifts to my mother. My mother was difficult to shop for. She didn't wear jewelry and didn't care about clothes. She was an excessively practical woman in every way. There wasn't a lot that existed that would make a good present for someone like her. My father was thoughtful enough to try, but most things went unused or were out-right failures. I'll give my dad credit; he always put forth a good effort, but his attempts to get his wife a proper gift were mostly flops. Except once. One Valentine's Day the old man hit an absolute grand slam by getting her something she loved. It would also be something that almost killed her.

My father had bursts of creativity at times. I was sitting in the living room one day when my parents came home with a small glass aquarium that had been fully decked out for some kind of animal living inside it.

"What's that?" I asked.

"Your father bought me two iguanas for Valentine's Day."

"You're kidding."

My father was beaming. I'd never seen him so proud of himself. He was feeling like a million bucks, you could tell. The old man had finally gotten a present for my mother that she loved. His self-worth was through the roof because of her excitement. The strange thing to me was that my father was not an animal lover, not at all. The guy had little to do with the pets we already owned. He never had anything to do with the cat and he seemed perpetually annoyed by the dog. I'm not sure that the reality of having two tropical lizards living with us had set in. Needless to say, he was not a man known for his powers of foresight. Either way, we had two new exotic pets, and he was feeling on top of the world. He had pleased my mother on this Valentine's Day and that was all that mattered. Mission accomplished.

Before we knew it, the aquarium was placed in my parents' office and "Great Beast" and "Maggie" became our two new reptilian family members. They started out small, about the size of a hot dog, then they grew. After a few months, it was apparent we had to buy a bigger aquarium. They continued to grow, and a few months later, we realized we had to buy a sofa-sized crate to house the animals. Within a year they had gotten to be five feet long. I'm positive my father had no idea these two little dinosaurs would grow that big when he initially bought them. I'm also sure he didn't realize that my mother would develop the habit of taking them out of their cage and letting them roam around the house. It was like living in the reptile house at the zoo.

It was not uncommon to be going from room to room and having either Maggie or Great Beast scamper in front of you. Without fail, this would scare the shit right out of you. We learned to live as if we were in a jungle, waiting for an exotic animal to attack. Everyone, except my mother, hated this but it became a way of life. On the plus side, it certainly made for a good conversation piece when nervous guests came over. It reminded me of something out of *The Addams Family*.

Giving animals their names is always an interesting part of pet ownership. The kids almost always have a lot of input. Most of the time, the entire family bats around a lot of ideas until a moniker is finally agreed upon. Then the animal lives its life constantly hearing the agreed upon syllables. The iguanas earned their names based on a combination of how they looked and their temperaments. Maggie was docile, mild-mannered, plump, and always serene. She was almost always found hugging a large branch set up in the corner of the office. You could hold a piece of iceberg lettuce in front of her and she'd slowly munch on it, like a calm little prehistoric dinosaur. She was cool and I liked her; I had different feelings for Great Beast.

If you can imagine the aggressive posture and attitude of a Tyrannosaurus rex, you'd have a good idea of what Great Beast was like. She was scrappy and seemed like she was always looking for a fight. There was an evil glint in her eyes. Her body was muscular and sinewy and she was sly and disturbingly fast. I had seen the movie *Aliens* and she reminded me of the terrifying creatures in that film. Most pets mature and become calm with age. This wouldn't be the case with her; with age she became lethal. There is no doubt that Great Beast had the mindset of a serial killer. Everyone, except my mother, was terrified.

One day, our fears came true. Great Beast committed murder.

We found the torn apart body of Maggie under the floor of her beloved branch. Blood was everywhere. The crime scene provided every bit of evidence we needed to put the pieces together. Poor Maggie, like a plant-eating brontosaurus, was hugging her tree limb. She had been minding her own business when something in the primitive brain of Great Beast snapped. She decided that it was killing season and climbed Maggie's limb to tear her innocent counterpart to pieces with her sharp, serrated jaw. It must have been a painful death. Poor, poor Maggie.

I'll never forget entering the room and looking over the horrifying crime scene. This was primal animal instinct at its scariest. The unforgiving law of the jungle had played itself out in my parents' office and Great Beast was now perched on her victim's branch. The tree limb would never be clung to by Maggie again. Her mutilated body now lay underneath her killer as Great Beast stared down with dominance. Blood covered everything. Maggie was not sleeping. Maggie was dead. It was survival of the fittest in the domestic world of civilized life.

We buried the murder victim in the backyard. There was no trial, but Great Beast had been found guilty. There was no precedent for dealing with this. What is a family supposed to do with a pet that has murdered another pet? My mother insisted that the reptilian murderer was still part of the family and we'd have to continue to care for her. Her love of animals left us with no choice. We simply moved on with life knowing we had a killer living amongst us. Then, one day, the killer escaped.

I read a lot of Stephen King novels when I was a kid. I was obsessed. His magic worked on me every time I'd pick up one of his books. Within a few pages I was sucked into a world of terror and surprise. His stories were visceral experiences and you felt them deep inside your bones. To me, they were like instruction manuals on how to deal with my own terrors and traumas. I'll forever be indebted to Stephen King and how much he gave me through his wonderful stories. In my opinion, *Pet Semetary* is his most frightening book. What would occur with Great Beast, after her escape, reminded me of this novel.

In the book, a father discovers an old Native American burial ground in his back woods. After his family's beloved cat is hit by a car, he buries it in the titular "Pet Semetary." Then, all hell breaks loose. Surprise! It turns out that burying something on these grounds results in pet zombies. The re-animated cat comes back to life…sort of. It returns to the family but it's not the same. It smells like death and is no longer a loving and friendly lap cat. This new version is a demonic, undead entity of evil.

This is kind of what happened with Great Beast. Like I said, she escaped. She was gone for months and we had come to the logical conclusion the demon lizard had died out in the back woods behind our house. It was interesting, in a Darwinian way, to imagine an iguana roaming around on its own in a natural environment that is different from its ideal habitat. I, for one, found her disappearance as cause for celebration. Call me crazy but I never liked the thought of living with lizards as pets from the very start. It always felt like a recipe for disaster. Now, both creatures were gone and only a giant crate in my parents' office remained to remind us of their existence.

Great Beast had vanished in May. The summer months went by, and autumn came. One day, my mother was driving down our road and noticed something sitting on the roof of the house. It was approximately five feet long from head to tail, it was green, it was muscular and sinewy, and it had an aggressive posture. Whatever it was, it seemed angry and unapproachable. Upon closer inspection it turned out to be an animal we all knew. Surprise! It was Great Beast. Was she back from the dead? I'm not sure. But, like the cat in *Pet Semetary*, she came back to us *different*. She had been evil before. We would soon find that her evil had amplified. Whatever happened during those months in the wild had turned her feral. The reptile was a killer before. Now she was something even more terrifying, untamed viciousness, and she would be out for blood for the remainder of her days. Great Beast had become a reptilian version of the Terminator.

Unfortunately, my Dr. Doolittle-like mother did not have the ability to comprehend this. She climbed a ladder, picked up Great Beast from the roof, climbed down and brought her back to her crate.

You can imagine everyone's surprise at the news.

"Great Beast is back!" exclaimed my mother.

Nobody shared her excitement. There was no protest we could make. My mother was too ecstatic about this miraculous survival story. Instead, we went back to life with a killer exotic animal in the house.

One day, later that winter, I fully realized the danger we were in. I came home from school to find the murderous iguana in the middle of the living room. Either it had escaped its crate or had been left out. It doesn't really matter. She was out and had been crawling around the house for a few hours on her own. The dog and the cat were nowhere to be found and neither were any of my family members. It was just me and Great Beast alone in the house.

I stood there looking at her, not sure what to do.

"Hi."

She only responded by slowly turning her head and looking at me with demon eyes. The eyes were telling me something. The message was unmistakable and terrifying.

"I'm going to kill you," was being broadcast to me from across the room from the glare of this pet from Hell.

I'm not an expert on the body language of reptiles, but the posture of Great Beast could only be described as "attack mode." My fight or flight instinct kicked in immediately. I wasn't sticking around. Fearing for my life, I looked for an escape route. The stairs were right in front of me so I bounded up them figuring the lizard would have a difficult time navigating a flight of steps. I was wrong.

I found myself furiously running for my life as if in a deadly game of tag. I could only hear the scratching noise her claws made as she chased me up the stairs. Adrenaline kicked in at the sound of murderous intent behind me. She was literally right on my heels when I reached the top of the stairs. Without turning back, I ran across the landing to my bedroom and reached the threshold of the door. The iguana was racing across the landing toward me. Terror struck my heart. This was not a nightmare. I was being attacked by the family pet. I was going to be killed by a god-damned iguana. This is not how I pictured my death, thanks a lot mom and dad. I slammed the door as quickly as I'd ever slammed a door. The next thing I heard was the sound of a fully grown iguana hopped up on its own feral insanity splatting against the door. I looked down to see its claws trying to scrape at me at the bottom of the door. The intensity of the clawing still gives me nightmares.

Pure instinct was guiding me and self-preservation was everything at this point. There was no lock on the door, so it would need to be barricaded. A full-sized dresser would do. I suddenly found myself all alone in my room, trapped. Soon, with some effort, there was a two-hundred-pound dresser and a bedroom door separating me from an animal that was trying to kill me. Sweat was pouring down my face and I was out of breath, but I was alive. Then came a terrible thought. What about my family? Where were they? Did the iguana kill them? Your imagination can go wild after being violently attacked by an animal.

I spent the next hour holed up in my bedroom like Butch Cassidy surrounded by the Bolivian Army. I was going to have to wait this siege out. There was no way I was opening my door to risk the threat of having my throat torn out by the killing machine we considered a household pet. After waiting in my barricaded bedroom for an hour I found that my family had not been killed. They were just shopping for groceries. My mother called my name from the bottom of the stairs.

"Brendy?"

"I'm in my room."

I removed the barricade and came out from hiding. It was imperative to let them know of the danger we were all in. I opened the door to find my mother standing on the other side. Great Beast was perched on her shoulder nuzzling her face. The monster was cozying up against my mother's cheek acting like she hadn't just assaulted me.

"That thing tried to kill me."

My mother was maddeningly dismissive. She refused to believe me and was unfazed. After listening to my story and my warnings, she defended the animal and walked away. I stood in astonishment. Some people can only believe what they choose to believe. My mother saw only the good in animals. Despite what I told her, she had a blind spot for the possibility of evil in one of God's creatures. The iguana, lounging on her shoulders, looked at me with smugness. She knew my mother had taken her side. The demon pet also seemed to be telling me something; a message was being transmitted from her reptilian eyes. *This wasn't over.* Her reign of terror would continue. Little did I know the animal's next victim would be the one person who defended the killer the most, my own mother.

"Don't bite the hand that feeds you" is a phrase I heard many times growing up. I'm not sure if I remember the exact contexts for which it was used. I just know I heard it a lot. It's obviously metaphorical advice about showing gratitude to something or somebody that takes care of you. For many years, my mother was literally the hand that fed her iguanas. She loved them and made them part of her daily routine. She kept their heat lights on and made sure they had a happy little lizard lifestyle. Maggie had been murdered, sure. That was Great Beast's fault. My mother's capacity for love of animals allowed her to turn the other cheek and keep loving Great Beast despite her flaws. She was the Mother Teresa of animals. But, as far as I know, Mother Teresa was never viciously attacked by the people she loved. In the end, Great Beast would prove to have zero gratitude for her caretaker.

One day, while at college, I received a phone call from my father.

"Brendan, you need to come home. Your mother's been attacked by that god damned iguana."

"What?"

"We should have put that friggin' thing down a long time ago."

"How's mom?"

"That little piece of crap nearly tore her finger off."

"What?"

"She might lose it. I've never seen anything like it."

He went on to tell me that my mother had reached into the cage to feed Great Beast when the animal suddenly went berserk and chomped down on her index finger. Its serrated jaw was powerful enough to do some real damage. Not only was the finger nearly severed, but the bacteria from an exotic animal could be lethal. Her bony digit had swelled to the size of an Italian sausage. She was treated at the hospital and given giant pills to fight the infection that might threaten her life. My father told me he needed me to come home to help deal with the animal. A duty had fallen on my shoulders because I was the only one in the family, other than my mother, willing to handle Great Beast. I didn't like doing it but neither my father nor my brothers would go near the thing. Now it was *my* job to go home and see to its destruction.

I met my parents in their living room a few hours after my father's call. My mother's hand was surrounded by a giant bandage. She was mournful. My father was a few drinks in and swearing up and down.

"We should have never bought those god-damned things" was the phrase he kept repeating.

My mother was beside herself. She knew Great Beast needed to be destroyed and could say nothing to protect the killer she had been harboring for the last few years. I wasn't there to be the executioner, that would be the job of the local veterinarian. My job would be more like that of a prison guard on death row. I was responsible for escorting the "dead-animal-walking" to its death.

This wasn't going to be an easy task because the iguana was hostile to everything. It was my job to reach into the cage, pick the damned thing up, get it into a plastic bin, and slam the lid shut. I imagined it would be like wrestling an angry alligator. The vet had been called and was expecting the animal within the hour. I put on the long industrial-strength rubber gloves that we used for picking the animal up. They were heavy duty and would be the only defense I had against being bit. I certainly didn't want to lose a finger or find myself taking horse pills to fight a rare tropical infection.

My mother stood beside me. Her job was to open the top of the iguana's crate. This was going to be intense and I had to be on top of my game. The crate was opened and I quickly reached down and seized the animal. Just as I imagined, the thing put up a hell of a fight. I grabbed her muscular torso with both hands while she did everything she could to escape my grasp. Her long tail violently whipped against me. Her neck was spasming from side to side trying to bite me. Her sinewy body writhed in my hands as I carried her out of the crate and threw her into the blue storage bin. My mother, with bandaged hand, swiftly put the lid on the bin as we heard Great Beast's claws scratching frantically from within trying desperately to get out. The hard part was over.

We drove to the vet and met the receptionist at the desk.

"Is this the exotic?" she asked.

"Yep, she's all yours." I handed over the bin.

The vet came out and explained how they would use a *humane* procedure to end Great Beast's life. They would use gas to execute the animal.

"She won't be in pain or feel a thing."

I didn't care. The thing tried to kill my mom. Its reign of terror was over. The demon lizard would be exorcised from our lives, and we could finally move on from the worst pet we ever had.

They say the death of childhood pets is a healthy way to prepare a kid for coping with mortality. It's a way to learn about the grieving process. The death of each iguana had minimal impact on me. I didn't shed a tear for either animal. I can't say that I learned anything about grieving from each loss. The death of our family dog was different.

As fate would have it, I found myself back in the same veterinarian's office only a few months later. Taking Great Beast there was fine. This time was very different. Our dog, Boz, had been a constant presence for most of my life. He had become old and was mostly blind and completely deaf. His puppy days were long gone and he was now grey and feeble. He'd always been somewhat of a pain in the ass, but we loved him anyway. He had always been there for us and he was almost always a good boy.

When I was a young college student it was not uncommon for me to find myself dog-sitting for my parents. They had gone away for the weekend and left me in charge of the house.

"Don't let the house burn down and keep the animals alive."

These were my only directions. The good news was that the house wouldn't go up in flames. I completely failed at the second task. That would be the bad news.

It was about eleven o'clock at night when I let Boz outside to do "his business." After five minutes I opened the door to let him back in, but he wasn't there. I waited a bit longer and opened the door again, but he was nowhere to be found. I spent the next few hours walking around the neighborhood calling out for him. This was stupid and futile because Boz was deaf, but I did it anyway. Eventually I gave up and went back to the house figuring somebody might have taken him in and I'd get a call in the morning.

The first thing I did when I woke up the next day was to walk around the neighborhood again looking for my poor, old dog. No luck. I went to the yellow pages and found the number for the animal control guy.

"Hello?"

"Hi. I'm looking for my dog. I let him out last night and he never came back."

"Was he old? Black and white markings?"

"Yes."

"Yep. I found that little guy half-frozen in a puddle down by the carwash."

"Was he dead?" I gulped.

"No. But he wasn't in good shape. I took him to the vet. You can find him there."

I felt sick. What did "he wasn't in good shape" mean? I jumped in the car and headed to the same veterinarian's office that had recently seen to the death of Great Beast. On my drive, I had a bad feeling. I knew this was going to be the last time I was going to see Boz.

When I entered the foyer of the local vet, the lyrics to Eric Clapton's "Tears in Heaven" were playing from a small overhead speaker in the room. You've got to be kidding me.

It was like the soundtrack to a movie to go along with the moment that every pet owner fears…having to put an animal down.

The vet met me in the waiting room and ushered me down a hallway into a room full of animal crates. There was Boz. He was in one of the crates. As soon as he saw me, he began crying and pawing at the metal cage. I knelt to pet him and tell him it was going to be okay. The vet opened the crate, but Boz didn't move. He only looked up at me with fear in his old eyes. He was terrified and shaking but he was so glad to see me. My old dog couldn't stop crying.

"He suffered significant nerve damage last night being out in the cold for so long. His back quarters are paralyzed."

My heart sunk hearing this. Nerve damage. Paralyzed.

The vet went on to explain how Boz's quality of life would never be the same. Eventually he got to the news I was anticipating.

"It's your choice, but I would recommend putting him down. He's an old dog and you'd be preventing him from suffering."

I nodded. I knew that the merciful thing was to let Boz go.

I called my parents, still on their weekend vacation, to let them know I had let them down and Boz was going to be put to sleep in the next few minutes. My mother cried. My father only told me that it had to be done.

The vet prepared me for what was next.

"I'm going to give him two shots. The first will calm him down. The second shot will stop his heart. You can leave if you'd like, or, you can stay and be with him."

I stayed.

I held Boz's face and looked in his eyes. I remembered him as a puppy when Jubby first brought him home. I remembered how little he was and how little we all were. It had been so long ago. I remembered how he was always begging for somebody to play with him. I thought of all the times he slept in bed with me, and I remembered how he would bark all the time and how it would piss off my old man, but that would just make us laugh. I remembered the wet nose kisses and the wagging tail we received whenever we came home. Boz had always been there. He wasn't just part of the scenery; he was one of us. At all our family dinners he sat at our feet begging for food. He watched us grow through elementary school and all the way through high school. He greeted us at the door thousands of times. We'd always pet his head and say hi to him whenever coming into the house. He spent so many hours on the couch watching our TV shows with us. We were his family. He loved us and we loved him. He spent his whole life with us. These were going to be the last moments of his life and I wasn't sure if I was ready to say good-bye, but I also knew I didn't have a choice.

I would be the last thing he would see. I told him he was the best dog and that I loved him. With tears running down my face, I watched his eyes looking into my own. Slowly I saw him fade away. I could only tell myself one thing over and over.

"It's okay. It's okay. It's okay. It's okay."

14

"Art Freak" vs. "School of Hard Knocks"

"Don't let school get in the way of your education." – Anonymous Advice

My twin brother had dyslexia. I, on the other hand, excelled at reading. In fact, I loved it. I was never without a comic book or a novel in my back pocket growing up, but Jubby really struggled. From early on I realized that school was something I was good at and Jubby was not. From the age of five all the way through high school, he wrestled with being a "good" student. This would be especially hard for someone whose parents were both teachers and who had two academically gifted brothers. Talk about feeling like the black sheep. The irony is that Jubby was truly brilliant. Unfortunately, he was going to school at a time when teachers were trying to figure out the best way to help kids with dyslexia.

In first grade, I remember bringing a test home that went on the fridge because I had earned a good grade. Jubby had not done well on the same test. While mine went up on display for all to see, his went in the garbage as an object of shame. I was enormously empathetic to my brother's feelings. I took notice and decided then and there that school wasn't worth the effort. It made my twin brother feel bad. Therefore, it didn't deserve my attention.

I'm not sure how deliberate it was, but in first grade I started to do very poorly in school. I knew only one thing; school made the person I loved most in the world feel bad. So, screw school. Screw teachers. Screw textbooks. Screw homework. Screw it all. It made my brother feel awful; therefore, I wouldn't try. He was struggling and I loved him very much and didn't want him to suffer alone, so I began tanking everything. I stopped doing homework and earned low grades. It didn't matter to me. I was more than fine being lost in the fantasy world of my comic books. My parents eventually took notice and talked to me. My response wasn't terribly articulate.

"You can do better than this. What's going on?"

"I don't know."

I said "I don't know" a lot as a kid. It was passive-aggressive, but it seemed to get adults off your back better than anything. Truthfully, I really didn't know. I couldn't explain what was going on with me. I feared getting in trouble if I told them I was intentionally doing poorly to protect Jubby's feelings. This came to a head at the end of our fourth-grade year when my parents had to make a wrenching decision. They saw Jubby having a difficult time and they saw that his struggle was causing me not to try. The situation had been properly diagnosed. It was a crisis, and something had to be done. There was only one solution.

When you're a kid there's nothing scarier than the thought of failing a grade. You might as well put a sandwich-board on a kid labeling him as retarded. Everybody will see you as a dummy and probably say it to your face. The feeling of it goes beyond embarrassment. Furthermore, it will last forever. You'll never be able to get around the fact that you failed a grade, and the world will think of you as a moron for the rest of your life.

For somebody who has a twin brother who didn't fail, it's far worse. Your twin is a living reminder of your own inadequacy. The one who continues his education is "the smart one" while the one who is held behind will always be "the stupid one." Making Jubby repeat fourth grade was not an easy choice and it almost ripped my mother apart. Throughout the years, she would say it was one of the hardest decisions she ever had to make. There was tremendous worry that this would cause irreparable psychic damage to her son. Regardless, a decision was made, and it wouldn't be reversed; there was no turning back.

The week before school ended, my parents asked Jubby and me to sit down. They needed to talk to us. Immediately we knew something was wrong. The first thought was that we were in trouble for doing something stupid. However, this meeting had a different tone. This was very serious. It was apparent that they didn't know how to break some news to us. I'd never seen either of my parents like this. They knew Jubby and I were close. We were "The Twins." They knew I loved to read and had academic aptitude, despite my lack of academic success. They knew Jubby needed help and moving him along was probably not a good thing for him. They also knew Jubby was very intelligent, but school was not a great place for a kid like him. They had made an agonizing decision and now they needed to tell us.

I'm sure there was a sensitive build-up they used to soften the blow. The only words that really stand out in my memory came from my mother.

"Jubby, we need to hold you back," she said with tears in her eyes.

"What?" Both of us said it.

We were in shock. It was beyond belief. This was the worst news ever. Jubby and I were paralyzed with sickness. We were flooded with desperation. Along with so many terrible feelings came a blitz of questions and panicked statements. Both Jubby and I, in tears, just lost it.

"People are going to think I'm retarded."

"We'll never see each other."

"What about my friends?"

"Fail me too."

"I'll try harder. Please don't do this. I'll learn to read better."

"Don't do this."

"I want to die."

This went on for hours. We cried until we were spent, all of us. In the end, a decision was made and there was no turning back. The original plan for us to go through school in the same grade had been changed and the future would be forever altered. That entire summer would be spent with worry and questions being asked. What would it be like going back to school in the fall? Many discussions took place at the kitchen table. They were more like pep talks about how things would end up being great. Every other night would involve one or both of our parents sitting us down to tell us inspirational stories. The message was clear. They were trying to assure us everything would be okay. We weren't sure.

Jubby was told that he should be excited about a chance to make new friends while I was taken aside and reminded it was going to be important for me to start trying harder in school. I was told that it was okay to try at school and I didn't need to protect Jubby's feelings anymore by doing poorly. Eventually the summer came to an end. I began fifth grade without my brother and Jubby stayed in fourth grade to do it all over again.

Kids are tough. Jubby was one of the toughest kids you could ever meet. Sure, he was physically strong, but his ability to get kicked in the teeth and keep going was monumental. In the end, he repeated fourth grade and did in fact make new friends whom he would have for life. I'd like to say that the stigma of failing didn't have too devastating an impact, but he would end up carrying the psychological wounds of failing a grade for a long time. Throughout middle and high school, he and I found ourselves becoming individuals and losing the identity of "The Twins." It happened gradually but by the time we were in upper grades, we had established ourselves as separate people.

While Jubby busted his ass to overcome his dyslexia, I developed a problem of my own, low-grade obsessive-compulsive disorder. I became fixated on the idea of achievement. Suddenly, I began really caring about school. My previous lack of concern and effort transformed into a slightly unhealthy determination. In seventh grade, I literally wrote a contract with myself on a piece of paper. What kid does that? The written statement was a promise that I would never allow myself to get a grade below a 90 average again. By eighth grade, I became obsessed with the idea of getting into a good college. By ninth grade, I had developed an anxiety filled routine that would follow me throughout my academic career.

To an outsider I must have given the impression that I had my shit together. That was the outward appearance, inside I was in a constant state of panic; perpetually worried about grades or sports or girls or my future or pleasing other people. I learned to live with anxiety, but I had to hide it; I was ashamed of it. It was embarrassing and made me feel weak. Other people didn't seem to be so concerned with getting good grades or getting into a good college. I pretended to be nonchalant but, truth be told, I was a wreck. A nervous breakdown felt like it was almost inevitable. Worse, admitting to these feelings didn't seem like a viable option. People would think I was crazy. Just keep it to myself. Suck it up, wimp. That's what I told myself.

It was art that saved me. I had always been good at drawing and always loved reading. Comic books offered escape and drawing was my therapy from the time I was in kindergarten. My friends loved to hunt and play sports. I loved playing sports, but hunting animals wasn't really my bag. *Art* was. None of my friends liked to read books or draw. They would tease me, lovingly I think, by referring to me as "an art freak." It didn't bother me. It was just their way of acknowledging my identity. Teenage lingo has always been code and there was nothing offensive to me about my friends calling me an "Art Freak." As hard as it is to believe, it meant "we love you."

Despite, and probably because of my acute hidden neurosis, I found myself going to a good college. My hard work paid off and I found myself getting an old-fashioned liberal arts education spending all my time painting, drawing, writing, and reading books. That suited me well. After all, I was an "art freak." Meanwhile, Jubby bravely fought his way through high school and heroically overcame his dyslexia. School was never for him but he stiff-upper-lipped it and graduated. Following graduation he attempted college; it didn't go very well. After attempting two semesters at a community college and failing out, he found himself back home and somewhat adrift. While I was at a university being an "art freak" he was experiencing the "school of hard knocks" stocking shelves in a grocery store by day and bartending at night. Despite having gone in two different directions and having widely different degrees of "success" we were both grappling with the same thing: What are you going to be when you grow up? Who are you? What's your purpose in life? Lots of people would look at me and ask, "So what are you going to do with all this artsy fartsy stuff?" Jubby would receive similar questions about his future. "What's next?" Neither of us knew.

The stark difference between our educational situations was always apparent. Despite being twins, we had always known how different we were. As young men who were not yet adults, we respected our differences. That didn't mean there wouldn't be occasions for those differences to create odd situations. My "artsy" college existence would sometimes mix with his "small-town-blue collar" lifestyle with ridiculous results. The different paths our so-called "educations" had taken us were never more apparent than the night he caught me naked in my bedroom with only a piece of chalk in my hand.

By far, and not for the most obvious reasons, the best class I ever had in college was called *Figure Drawing*. It was a three-hour class that took place once a week for fifteen weeks. The basic premise of the class was simple; a group of "artsy fartsy" students sat in a circle with easels in front of them drawing naked women. It was an amazing class. Yeah, I know, I got to spend three hours a night staring at beautiful naked women, but I also learned a lot about myself and grew as an artist. Isn't that what going to college is all about?

I was living in a fraternity house at the time, and coming home from class would almost always involve my fraternity brothers begging to see the pictures of naked women I had just spent three hours sketching. It was surreal. I was being sent to college to draw women with absolutely no clothing on. This seemed like the very definition of getting a "quality liberal arts education." I didn't know what job would be available for me after college but, at the time, I didn't care. The semester rushed by as I continued to stuff my portfolio with hundreds of sketches of bare-naked ladies. Towards the end of the semester, the professor announced there was going to be a final exam. What the hell? How does one take a final exam for a figure drawing class? Then, he proceeded to hand us all a rolled-up sheet of six-foot-long black paper. After that, he handed us a few pieces of white chalk.

"Your final exam is to do a life-size drawing on this black sheet of paper with only white chalk. Your model will be yourself…. *naked.*"

Oh no. Seriously? Outside of my naked mother, I can't think of another thing that I would want to draw less than my own nude body. Drawing a full-sized nude portrait of myself in my birthday suit was a terrible problem. I just really, really, really didn't want to do it. I didn't even like being naked for the three or four seconds I stepped out of the shower. This was going to involve a good chunk of time where I stood in a room without a stitch of clothing on my body. Also, the entire process sounded like a logistic nightmare. Think, for one second, about what the project would entail. You would have to get a big mirror. You would have to find a space for total privacy. You would have to pin the black paper to the wall. You would have to strip down completely naked as you spent hours looking at your body in the mirror and trying to render it on a giant piece of paper. Did I mention it was supposed to be life-size? Not a single part of this activity was appealing. I walked home from class with a roll of black paper under my arm and white chalk in my hand. My mind was very busy as I walked home figuring out the logistics of my assignment. One thing was for sure, I didn't feel like I could confide in anyone. For some reason, I was too embarrassed. Also, if my friends knew there was going to be a six-foot-tall portrait of my naked body, it could be used as blackmail. I wasn't sure I could trust anybody with my dilemma.

I was all alone with my problem, and in the end, I was going to have bite the bullet and draw my own naked body. There was no getting around it and I needed to have a plan. It would be impossible to do this in a fraternity house. I would need to head home for the kind of privacy this task required. After some contemplation, I devised a strategy. I figured I could wait until my parents went to bed, prop up an old mirror, get undressed, and start sketching like a madman. Jubby, who lived at home, would be busy as he spent his nights bartending until about 2:30 in the morning. The plan was solid and I thought I just might be able to pull it off.

My parents went to bed around 10 o'clock that night. As soon as I heard my father snoring, I went to work. The black paper was pinned up. With chalk in hand, I began sketching my head. After a short time, I had rendered a floating likeness of myself that was staring back at me. My drawn expression couldn't hide how nervous I was at what I was about to do. I decided to just keep going. Come on, get it over with. I took my shirt off. It might be best if I did this in pieces. I furiously drew my torso and my arms. My focus was fueled by the fear of my folks waking up and walking into my room to discover me in the buff with a little piece of chalk in my hands. What a narcissist our son has become! The shame might be too much to bear.

Before long, my chalked head and torso were staring at me. The lower half still needed to be drawn to prop up the upper half. I took the Nike motto and *just did it*. Suddenly I'm pulling off my shoes, my socks, and my jeans. I still had my boxers on as I endeavored to draw my feet, ankles, calves, and thighs. I was saving the worst for last. I stepped back to look at the strange sight of a six-foot-tall chalk drawing of myself staring back at me. The body was fine, however, there was a strange expression on the face staring back at me. The feelings of embarrassment, amusement, shame, and fear were apparent. My emotions had been captured with astonishing accuracy. However, the drawing was incomplete. I looked like a eunuch. Ughhhhhh, I still had to draw my private parts.

Just get it over! Do it!

I'm sweating. I look at the clock. It's just after midnight. My bartending brother won't be home for a couple more hours. My parents are fast asleep and I'm almost done. I can see the finish line. Keep going. Let's just get this over. Suddenly my boxers are on the bed and I'm staring at my own man-parts trying to figure out exactly how to go about sketching them on this piece of paper. A few minutes of delirious chalk strokes and the drawing is complete. I'm fully naked staring at an equally fully naked version of myself hanging on the wall. I did it! Whew. It was over. Mission accomplished.

That's when I heard the front door open.

Oh, shit! It's Jubby. He came home from the bar early. Oh, shit. I hear him running up the stairs very quickly. Oh, shit. He's headed right for my bedroom. Oh, shit. I have no time to do anything at all. I'm frozen in a state of balls out naked panic. Literally. My brother gets to the top of the stairs and looks into my room to see me entirely nude with a stricken expression on my face. This wasn't a sight he was expecting.

"What the hell are you doing?"

Then he saw the black paper on the wall with my freshly drawn nude body staring at him as well with a slightly less mortified look on its face.

"What the hell is that?"

I really wish I'd had the suave nature at twenty years old to confidently stand unclothed in that room and say something like, "I'm drawing myself naked. What's it look like? Shut the door, why don't ya!"

I just wasn't cocky enough to do that. Instead, I reacted out of panic and embarrassment and proceeded to have an argument with my brother while I was completely in the buff.

"Don't tell anybody."

"Oh, man. No way. I'm telling everybody!"

"Come on. Please."

"Dude, this is some serious art freak shit going on."

"It's for a final exam in my class," I explained.

"What the hell kind of college are you going to? And can you put some friggin' clothes on already?"

He did, in fact, tell everybody. I can't blame him. It was a funny story and I had no defense; I got caught drawing myself in the buff. But it was for the sake of my art, and in the end, I was happy to be sacrificed at the altar of my friends' loving mockery. They were actually very kind to me after hearing about the incident and I took some ribbing, but they understood, and it was worth the laughter. We all had our roles to play within our group. I was the "art freak."

The good news was that I had successfully completed the final. I took my rolled-up black sheet of paper and dropped it off on the professor's desk along with all the other final exams from students in the class. While handing my project in, it dawned on me how weird this assignment was. I imagined my teacher unfurling all the naked bodies of the students who sat in his class that semester. It seemed a little serial killer-ish to me. Imagine a man taking dozens of life size portraits to his home, pinning them up in his basement and "grading" them. Gross and weird.

Despite the agony of having to go through this ordeal, there *was* a happy ending. The professor had graded the "exams" and we were to pick them up in his office. He put the black scrolled masterpiece into my hands and thanked me for working hard during the semester.

"I'm looking forward to seeing you next semester in Figure Drawing II."

"I'll bet you are," I thought but didn't say.

When I got to the hallway the temptation was too much. I had to see the grade he had given me. I began unrolling the artwork in my hands. I immediately saw the grade: A+. Fantastic! But the best part was the comment under the grade: "VERY IMPRESSIVE!!" The "Art Freak" got the last laugh.

As I finished my college education to find my calling as a teacher, Jubby continued going to the "School of Hard Knocks." He spent a lot of time hustling, bartending, working in a grocery store, and doing any odd jobs he could find. There was no school to get in the way of his education. He was adrift in the sea of young adulthood with lots of questions and too many unknowns. Finding yourself might be the hardest part of growing up, but those were necessary years for both of us to do a lot of soul-searching.

Despite a lot of worry, it didn't take long for Jubby to find the path he was meant to take. The idea of criminal justice was appealing to him. He always had a strong sense of right and wrong and he wasn't afraid of anything, ever. It kind of seemed like a no-brainer. He first went to the Corrections Academy and immediately decided that watching prisoners all day for twenty years was going to be a tough gig. However, for the first time in his life he had gone to a school and done well. Law enforcement suited him, and he was thriving. What a relief. The success carried on as he immediately went to the Police Academy and within a year, found himself a full-fledged officer of the law. He was a cop. Suddenly, everything made a lot of sense.

He had come a long way from the little kid who was held back in fourth grade. He had overcome dyslexia and the stigma of flunking a grade. He didn't let those setbacks define him and I couldn't have been prouder of him. After his graduation, I remember seeing him in his uniform for the first time. I thought back to the day my parents sat us down to tell him he was going to repeat fourth grade.

"You did it," I said.

"*We* did it."

We weren't really huggers, but we hugged each other that day.

We would always be twin brothers who shared so many of our experiences. Eventually we had to go in different directions to find our own purpose. Our differences had always defined us. The quiet one and the rowdy one. The dark-haired one and the blonde one. The kid who loved reading and the kid who struggled with school. Our differences had caused our lives to take different paths. How could they not? His "hard knocks" education led him to be a cop while my "artsy" ways would lead me into a teaching career. We both found our calling despite it all and everything turned out okay.

15

King of the Beach

There's nothing like having brothers. Mine gave me a lot of things. They certainly gave me an endless amount of torment and persecuted me beyond belief. The Spanish Inquisition had nothing on the torture techniques of my siblings. Their cruelty could be jaw-dropping. Growing up in my household was a bit like a *Lord of the Flies* experience. From one moment to the next we could all turn into savages. There was a sense of fear and you always had to be on guard. You never knew when there might be a sneak attack or a prank that might be pulled. My fight or flight instincts were sharpened by the existence of my brothers.

On the other hand, Aran and Jubby also gave me endless amounts of joy and happiness. Nobody would ever make me laugh harder than my brothers. In the great school of life, they would prove to be my best teachers. They taught me how to be tough; how to suck up pain and not be soft, and how to fight through hardship. But the most important lesson I received from them could be summed up in one phrase: When it comes right down to it, don't take shit from anybody.

The three of us were expected to make money from as early as I can remember. My father pushed all of us to get out and start making a buck or two when we were old enough to push a mower around. Aran, being six years older, had the cool job of delivering newspapers around town on his bicycle. Always rather crafty, in a big brother way, he realized that his bicycle riding younger brothers would be eager enough to do the job for him without having the cleverness to feel entitled to the pay. We just thought it was cool to throw newspapers at people's doorsteps while peddling all around town. Aran was never above taking advantage of his naïve younger siblings.

Jubby and I eventually got jobs mowing random people's lawns. I lucked out in that department scoring a job mowing the town lawyer's lawn. He had a rider mower and he paid about thirty bucks a pop. Jubby ended up snagging a job from an old spinster who owned two acres and made him push mow the whole damned thing. She ended up only paying him about five dollars per job. Worse, she'd subract a nickel for every patch of grass he missed.

By the time we were eighteen we put lawnmowing behind us and became certified lifeguards. Aran had been working as a lifeguard at a local lakefront for about six years and thought it would be a good idea for his little brothers, now old enough, to work alongside him. Always good at playing follow the leader when it came time to do what our big brother did, we jumped at the chance and found ourselves working at a swimming area at a small local lake. It would be the summer job that would employ all of us for years. In many ways, it was a job that helped us become young men.

Nobody referred to where we worked as "The Lake." Instead, we called it "The Beach." It was owned, funded, and operated by the County. Therefore, we were County employees and servants of the so-called taxpayer dollar. When Aran started working at "The Beach," six years before Jubby and I ever got there, times were a little different. According to him, the early years were the "glory days" because there were no real rules. Legend had it there was a keg on constant tap in the guard house and lifeguards spent most days fighting sobriety instead of looking out for distressed swimmers. By the time Jubby and were hired, things were much more on the up and up. The hedonistic days of yesteryear were over, and the ship was shaped up. The "glory days" can't last forever.

The Beach truly was a beautiful place. Surrounded by rolling hills, the lake was a pristine location. Upscale cottages were scattered throughout the perimeter. Docks, lined with all sorts of fancy boats, jutted out into the water. It was a man-made lake and the water level was controlled by a dam. At the beginning of every spring, the dam would allow the lake to be filled and every fall the lake would be emptied. In the wintertime, the houses along the shore would overlook a depressing muddy wasteland. But in the summer, the place was glorious. The County Swim Area also acted as a park. There was a guard house in the center. Attached to each side of the guard house were men's and women's restrooms. There were bar-b-que pits and picnic tables dotted around the three acres of land. A parking lot separated the grassy picnic area from the section used for beach-like activity. Two lifeguard chairs sat about fifty feet from one another and looked out onto two acres of roped off water. There was a long, rectangular standing dock in the middle, a floating dock off to the right, and a square standing dock off to the far right. It was a timeless place; majestic and picturesque. The same cannot be said for the clientele.

"The Beach" was not always what I would call a family friendly place. It was certainly intended to be the kind of place that was friendly and safe. I'm sure the people who first envisioned the park imagined a peaceful setting where a mother and father could take their kids swimming on a hot summer day. Picture the middle-class American dream tumbling out of the family station wagon with picnic baskets and blow up floaties. This was the postcard ideal, but reality would prove to be quite different. Most people came to get drunk, get stoned, get in fights, and act like complete a-holes just for kicks. From day one, I would learn that the title of "lifeguard" involved way more than just protecting people from drowning. I also acted as a bouncer breaking up fist fights and an occasional knife fight. I was a groundskeeper who had to maintain the natural beauty of the park by mowing grass and raking sand. I also acted as custodian and had the duty of cleaning up diarrhea and used tampons from the bathroom floors. We were Swiss Army Knife employees. We did everything.

Our boss was one of the most influential people in our lives. His name was John Cosgrove, but we just called him Coz. Most people found him reprehensible, but we loved him. By most accounts, he was a dirty old man. In our view, he was just misunderstood. Coz was in his late fifties when I first met him. He was winding down his career as a high school Phys. Ed. Teacher. His adult children had moved out long ago and several years had passed since his divorce. In his younger years, he had been a star football player in college and went by the nickname "Fido." I had been warned not to call him that, ever. Apparently, he hated it. I never had the guts to try. He was a *true* football player, too. He played both ways. He was a skilled offensive-linemen on one side of the ball and a tremendous nose-tackle on the defensive side. Everything about the man was stocky. He had stocky legs, stocky fingers, stocky arms, and a stocky neck. Curly white hair covered his entire body. His summertime uniform consisted of a tank top, athletic shorts, and an assortment of gold jewelry that sat in a white, curly jungle of chest hair. He had a deep, raspy voice and a loud boisterous laugh. If Santa Claus had a cousin who grew up on the wrong side of the tracks, it might resemble Cosgrove. Coz loved a few things in life. He loved overseeing The Beach, drinking Miller High Life all day long, playing card games like *Skat* and *Casino*, and trying to pick up skanks from local bars. But he also loved me and my brothers as if we were his own sons. He got a kick out of us as much as we enjoyed him.

Aran, Jubby, and I worked with each other at The Beach for six summers in a row. It was a tough place to work and not for the faint of heart. The days were hot and long, and you never knew what to expect from a drunken crowd of summer revelers. The one thing we did know is that we were always glad to be working with one another. It was a job in which you'd need back-up, and the fact is, there is no better back-up than brothers.

The most memorable summer working at The Lake was the one when there was no water in it. It goes without saying that it's very difficult to do the job of a lifeguard when there is nowhere to swim. My third summer working at The Beach was by far the strangest out of all the years I was employed there. The previous winter saw almost no snowfall, therefore the water table in the ground was very low. There was also very little rainfall that year. This was a double whammy that would devastate lake-goers looking for aquatic recreation during the summer season. When the officials released the dam that year, it only filled the lake halfway. The swimming area had almost no water in it. It was a puddle. There was not a single drop of water surrounding any of the docks. What used to be a beautiful view was now a depressing sight. Our beautiful park had become an apocalyptic vision out of a *Mad Max* movie.

Our jobs would be very different that summer, that is, if we had jobs. We had to beg and plead with the County to convince them that safety personnel would still be necessary to keep things going at the swimming area. Thank God they agreed, and we would be able to make some much-needed money. I wasn't looking forward to working at a fast-food joint. Luckily that wouldn't happen, but our normal working routine would be very different from previous years working at the lake.

Instead of guarding from the vantage point of the chairs, we found ourselves standing at the top of a long rectangular dock surrounded by absolutely no water. It was a farce. All we did was blow our whistles and yell at kids not to pick up rocks from the dry lake-bottom and throw them at each other. Three months of total boredom and frustration was our cross to bear that summer. People who showed up looking to swim were immediately frustrated and temperamental. We spent a lot of time having to explain the scientific reason there was no water in the area where it should have been.

"Well, ain't that just the damndest thing," was usually how the response went, or some approximation of that sentiment.

The days were more than tedious, and we fought the monotony by playing a ton of card games in the guard house. I was never more thankful to be working with my brothers. We were always good at finding ways to entertain ourselves. Practical jokes and ribbing are necessary in making long, hot work hours go by more quickly. Sitting around and doing a lot of nothing turns out to be a difficult job, but we each had a wicked sense of humor that didn't let the boredom get ahead of us. Then the tedium was dramatically interrupted in the middle of the summer during the hottest day of the year. This would come to be known as "The Day of the Douche-Bags."

Aran, Jubby, and I were the lifeguards on duty that day. We were playing cards in the guard house that morning. Eventually people would show up and we would have to go out and police the puddle of water from rock-throwing maniacs. There was almost always tension in the air. You got used to it, but this day felt different. We had a sense something treacherous was waiting for us. It wasn't a good feeling. On hot summer weekends you could almost smell the potential for violence in the air and our hackles were up.

The first car that pulled in that day was a white Chevy S-10 truck. It had two passengers in the cab and about five shirtless young men hanging out of the truck bed. They had coolers full of beer and it was obvious that their break-fast that morning was of the liquid variety. We could tell they were complete a-holes from the get-go. We were experts in assessment. My brothers and I were all drinkers; a group of guys drinking wasn't a big deal, but these guys were the worst. They were amateurs, the typical weekend warriors all juiced up and ready to go. Their personalities were their own birth control. Adding alcohol to a bunch of jackasses like these guys never yields positive results.

Their first statement proved our first impression was accurate. It came from a shirtless pair of wrap-around sunglasses wearing a cockeyed baseball cap.

"Hey fellas, is this the spot where we can pick up some ass today?"

"What?"

The cut-off jeans continued, "Any women come here?"

"Yeah, if you're into stay-at-home moms with their kids."

Our new friend chuckled.

"So, my bros and I are gonna set up and drink brews all day long. We saw that there's a spot for playing volleyball but there's no net."

"We'll set up the net for you."

"Cool. Thanks *Chief.*"

And there it was. "Chief." This is a term that, used in this context, stands as proof that this guy and his entire brood of shirtless, arrogant weekend warriors were complete ass-hats. Of course, he called us "Chief." My brothers and I had come to know this archetype only too well. Usually, they would be guys that work retail in stores like *American Eagle* or *Abercrombie and Fitch*. They might also refer to you as "Big Guy," or "Boss," or something that sounds flattering but actually isn't. In fact, it's the opposite. Calling somebody "Chief," "Big Guy," or "Boss," is an act of condescension. It's a particular brand of cool-guy pos-turing and the calling card of world-class jerks that deserve to be kicked in the groin, repeatedly. The "Chief" standing in front of us asking to have the volleyball net set up was the poster boy for this kind of a-hole. I would have bet a thousand dollars on the spot that the guy would face several charges of date rape throughout his life.

Jubby and I carried the volleyball net out to the court and set it up while the "Dickstreet Boys" continued being loud and obnoxious.

"Thanks, Big Man," one of them said to Jubby as we were walking away.

We just looked at each other. Twin telepathy, at work again, told me what he was thinking. It was exactly what I was thinking. These guys were going to be a problem all day. With a shared eye roll we headed back to the guard house and continued playing cards.

The day, like all days that summer, moved rather slowly. A sizable crowd of people showed up to picnic and mill around the pathetic excuse for a swim area. Aran, Jubby, and I rotated our shifts in twenty-minute sections throughout the hours of the day. The guard who was on duty would stand atop the middle dock to look over the crowd and keep some semblance of order. In other words, we blew our whistles and yelled at kids not to throw rocks. We were paid eight dollars an hour for that. With no water surrounding it, the spot where we stood was a good fifteen feet in the air and overlooked a dry and desolate wasteland.

Mostly the events of the day had been typical, but there was still a bad feeling in the air. Our radar was buzzing. It was just one of those days where it felt like you were waiting for something bad to happen. Maybe it was the initial encounter with Chief and his gang. We were used to dealing with jerks and the guys playing volleyball were nothing to get too worked up about, just drunken morons. However, something seemed off about them and our sixth sense for trouble was sending definite signals.

Eventually the crowd thinned out as the sun was starting to set. One of the hottest days of that summer was almost over and I was pulling the final shift on top of the dock. Aran, Jubby and Coz were employed in the guard house in a serious game of *Skat*.

A few people were scattered below me milling around in the saddest-looking swimming area that ever existed when I looked over to the end of the dock and saw somebody climbing up the ladder. It was Chief, my buddy from earlier in the day. He reached the top and was now drunkenly stumbling my way.

"Only guards are allowed up here."

"Cool. Cool. I just gotta ask you a few questions Boss."

Ugghhh.

He sure stuck to the script and played the role of douche bag perfectly. The guy was staggering drunk. Behind him, his pack of thoroughly pickled buddies were piled into the flatbed of the truck aimed at the gate. The driver was revving the engine and they were all yelling for Chief to hurry up. They were really giving him a hard time.

"Let's go man! Come on! Let's go!" They called from the truck.

Chief just waved at them with a stupid grin on his face.

"Hold on guys. I'll be right there. I just gotta talk to my new friend here."

This guy was something else. I gave him no reaction, no emotion. There's no real talking with a guy like this. I just reminded myself to be professional and remain stone-faced. That's the only way to deal with arrogant pricks.

"So, what the hell happened to all the water, Boss?"

"Not enough snow and rain." Keep it short and sweet.

"Daaaaamn! That sucks, Bro."

The calls from his buddies grew louder and more impatient.

"Come on you pussy. Let's go!!"

"Yeah, yeah. One minute," Chief calls back.

To send a message of complete indifference, I walked away from him and stepped to the edge of the dock. I wanted my body language to send a message that even this moron could understand. I turned my back to signal that I was done talking with him. The honking from the truck escalated.

He circled behind me to look down over the other side of the dock. "Snap! There's no water over here either."

"No shit," I thought.

Then, boom! I felt a shove in the middle of my back and found myself flying through the air. I fell fifteen feet and landed on the hard rocks below. Boom! It happened so fast, but I immediately knew what had happened. This guy just Pearl Harbored me! I looked up from where I was lying to see him standing above me on the dock aiming two middle fingers down at me.

"F you!" (he didn't say 'F') he yelled and then disappeared to jump off the other side of the dock.

His joke was immediately apparent. He was going to get up on the dock, knock the lifeguard onto the rocks below, then he was going to jump down, run to the escape vehicle, hop on the back of the truck and he and his buddies were going to speed through the gates like the coolest guys that ever drank beer and played beach volleyball. What a fun, delightful little prank.

They had no idea how badly their master plan would fail. How could they have known they would be dealing with three brothers completely ready for their brand of ass-grabbing stupidity.

Before I had been pushed off the dock, Coz and my brothers had noticed that Chief had climbed atop the structure to have his little conversation with me. They were already on high alert when they witnessed me get pushed off. The three of them sprang into action like a god-damned S.W.A.T. team. Things couldn't have happened more perfectly.

Right after Chief flips me off, he jumps off the dock, and in his drunkenness, doesn't realize how high up he is. He lands on the ground and ends up either spraining or breaking his ankle. He then proceeds to limp-run in a panic to get to his escape truck. Totally enraged, I begin running on the opposite side of the dock to catch up with him. I'm about ten feet behind him, and I see his buddies frantically waving for him to hurry up. This piece of human vomit is limping severely, and I'm right on his heels. Then I see one of the coolest things I've ever seen. Chief attempts to jump the little fence that separates the beach area from the parking lot. In mid-hurdle I see a giant arm come out of nowhere and clothesline the bastard. Chief does a complete backward somersault in mid-air and lands on the ground only to have my twin brother, who just close-lined him, immediately wrap his gigantic arm around the guy's throat. Jubby starts choking the life out of him. Simultaneously, Aran gets to the driver of the S-10, grabs him by the throat and forcefully recommends that he not even think about driving. While this is happening, Coz gets to the gate, closes it and locks it up.

They were trapped.

Within a second, I got to Chief whose face was blood-red and his eyes were bulging out of their sockets. Jubby was killing him. Rational thought left me. The hulk inside me was about to come out. While Jubby choked him, I started hitting the guy in the face as hard as I could. I don't know how many times I hit him, but blood was coming out of the guy's nose and mouth. It was like a geyser. Every hit was like raw meat exploding under my fist. It was then I realized my car keys that were always attached to my lanyard were still in my hand. I had been belting the guy with the keys sticking through my fist.

Eventually, I stopped hitting Chief's face only to look up at a little girl, holding her father's hand, with an expression of amazement on her face. Entire families came to the beach that day to have picnics and engage in some summer family fun. Little did they know they'd be getting entertained by some top-notch World Wrestling Federation style violence. Groups of families surrounded us, not knowing what to do. It must have been shocking to see lifeguards engage in this kind of brutality. The lost innocence on the little girl's face made me gradually stop hitting Chief.

"Let him go before you kill the prick." Coz's gravelly voice yelled at us.

"No." Jubby was going to kill the guy.

"Jered. Let him go, now."

"No."

"Jubby, it's okay. Let him go." I said it. I was out of breath and still enraged but he was going to kill the guy.

Jubby looked up at me. He saw that I was fine and looked down at the piece of garbage he was strangling and released him. He had sufficiently taught the guy a lesson.

"Get in your truck and get the hell out of here. We got your license number. Don't even try showing your faces again."

Coz knew there was no more to be done. These guys were just run of the mill cowards. Worse, they were drunken cowards. They thought they were going to pull some sophomoric prank that they could brag about for the rest of their date-raping lives and they got caught. We unlocked the gate and let them drive away. When they got to the road, they peeled out and aimed a collective "F You" (they didn't say 'F') at all of us.

A few of the fathers who had witnessed the incident came up to us in complete disbelief. One of the men sheepishly approached Jubby.

"I thought you were going to kill that guy."

"I was. He pushed my brother off the dock."

Like I said, there's nothing like having brothers.

16

It's Okay

One of Dante's punishments in a circle of Hell must include an aggressively ringing phone while trying to sleep off a hangover. My alarm clock told me it was nine in the morning. My head was pounding from the previous night's revelries. It had been my older brother's bachelor party and his wedding was in six days. The phone stopped ringing and I rolled over with the pillow clutched around my head. The phone began ringing again. It must be important. I dragged my ass out of bed and attempted to hustle through a couple rooms to get to the phone.

"Hello."

"Beej. It's Mark." It was my best friend's father; the only one in my life who still called me by my little-kid nickname. Everyone else had decided to shorten it even further by just referring to me simply as "B." By the time you're in your mid-twenties certain things must change, nicknames are one of them.

"Do you think you can give me a hand getting the Church Hall ready for Aran's wedding reception?"

Mark, a carpenter and a jack of all trades, had spent years doing odd jobs for the church. Mark was a great guy. He was the kind of guy who always seemed like he was in pretty good spirits even on the worst of days. Bad luck seemed to follow the guy around like a curse, but he had an indefatigable soul. Mark's rotten luck also had a way of infecting other people who might be around him. For instance, Mark was the reason I stepped on a rusty spike in his front yard when I was ten. You might be inclined to say that Mark's lifetime of misfortune could indicate carelessness. That might be true, but I think it also had to do with just being unlucky. Either way, Mark was always a guy that could take his lumps and keep on going with a smile on his face. You had to love him for that.

"Sure, I can help you out."

 I couldn't say no. He was my best friend Patrick's father. More than that, though, was the code. The code was simple; help somebody else out if they need it. Nobody ever talked about it. It was just an idea that went along with being a man. While I grew up, I watched guys constantly doing things according to the code. I saw gruff and tough adult men go out of their way to help others out. Sometimes they'd assist complete strangers stranded on the side of the road and sometimes they'd help close buddies who needed a hand building a garage. If somebody asked you for help, you would do everything you could for them. It was a code; don't let another person down. Mark needed help with a job and, despite being hungover, I was more than happy to honor the code. Little did I know this decision would almost kill the both of us.

I met Mark outside the Church Hall. It was a large brick building that had been built in the 1940s. For decades it had been a multi-functional building. It hosted hundreds of roast beef dinners, fish fries, lawn fetes, magic shows, musical programs, and community meetings over the years. But it also functioned as a recreational gymnasium for the Catholic church. Its high ceilings and large size allowed it to be used as a basketball court. The floor was painted with two basketball keys. The windows were barred with heavy iron grates, to prevent balls from smashing through them. Two large basketball hoops faced each other on either side of the court. The hoops were, of course, connected to backboards that were attached to steel bars that were bolted to the cement walls.

"Beej. Here's what were gonna do." Mark had a thick Buffalo accent.

"Nobody plays hoops in here anymore and the whole place is eventually gonna get renovated. So, we're gonna fix the place up nice for your brother's wedding by taking the basketball hoops off the walls. That way it won't look like a friggin' gym in here for his big day."

"Okay."

I looked at the mounted backboards trying to figure out their weight. In total they looked like they might each have gone about five hundred pounds. It seemed like this might be a job for more than one guy in his mid-fifties and a younger guy nursing a bad hangover. In the end, I trusted that Mark knew what he was doing. I was good at taking orders, so I went along with his plan. What did I know?

I was right; the job was more appropriate for five or six grown men. The hoops were ridiculously heavy. It would've been difficult even if I wasn't hungover. Somehow, we were able to lower each to the ground. It wasn't smooth. Truth be told, we pretty much dropped each one to the hard-tiled floor of the gym. But after an hour of work, the Church Hall that acted as a basketball court for decades was suddenly without any hoops. I figured the job was finished and I had fulfilled the code for the day. My head was still pounding, and I was looking forward to getting back to my bed.

"What do you think about those metal grates?" Mark said pointing up at the windows surrounding the entirety of the Hall.

"What do you mean?" I asked.

"Well, it's not a gym anymore so the metal grates don't need to be there."

"I guess not."

"It kind of looks like a prison the way it is now."

"Yeah, I guess so."

"The wedding reception will look a hell of a lot better if we get those down…don't you think?"

Unfortunately, the question was rhetorical. It didn't matter what I thought.

I looked around the room. There were about sixteen windows near the top of the ceiling all with metal grates covering them. Each window was about thirty feet in the air and would require climbing the church's tall, rickety old ladders. The grates were screwed to the wall by rusty, old hinges. This was going to take a hell of a long time, but the code prevented me from saying no and I found myself agreeing to help take the metal grates off the windows. My life would be changed forever.

"Here's the plan. We get the two big ladders out. You 'A-Frame' yours out and climb to the top. All you gotta do is hold on to the grate. I'm gonna rest my ladder against the wall right next to yours and zip the screws out of the hinges with the old screw gun. Easy peasey."

It didn't sound "easy-peasey" to me. It sounded like a lot of work but, again, I couldn't say no to Mark.

Before long I found myself acting out his plan. I was perched, like a bird, on the top of the ladder clutching a metal grate that must have weighed a good fifty pounds. Mark's ladder rested against the wall as he zipped out screws from the hinges attaching the grate to the cement brick wall. When the grate was freed from its home, I carried it to the ground. One window took about ten minutes. One down, an ass-load more to go. This was going to take all afternoon. We adjusted the ladders for the second window. If only we'd decided to stop then and there, but we didn't.

Once again, I found myself thirty feet in the air precariously sitting on top of the world's oldest ladder, holding onto a metal grate. Mark continued to zip the screws from the cement wall. When he was taking out the final screw, something strange happened. I watched the screw come out and immediately knew what was going to happen next. Everything went into terrible slow motion. I looked over to see that Mark's ladder wasn't resting against the cement wall anymore. It was now resting against the metal grate he was unscrewing from the wall. In a nano-second, I did the math in my head. The equation told the future, and it wasn't going to be pretty, not by a long shot. It all flashed in my mind before it actually happened.

The final screw was going to come out. Gravity was going to cause the heavy grate to slip downward. The thirty-foot ladder Mark was standing on was going to slip along with it. In his descent, Mark and his ladder would undercut the ladder I was still perched on near the ceiling. I would then be completely upended, still holding the grate, as I fell headfirst toward the hard-tiled floor that had hosted so many roast beef dinners. Now, that same floor would offer nothing more than an inevitable collision for both Mark and me. In my descent I would have a sudden realization. The grate I was still holding, while falling, was going to impale me and possibly Mark who had already crashed onto the floor below me. In less than half a second, I would have to throw the grate to prevent it from killing both of us with its terrible threat of lethal impalement. Basic physics would tell anyone that it is very difficult for a hungover twenty-five-year-old man falling head-first from a tall ladder to obtain the proper momentum necessary to heave a fifty-pound metal grate in the middle of his descent. Nonetheless, I would toss the object to the best of my ability. It wouldn't travel far but my attempt proved successful; neither of us would be impaled by its sharp corners. It would be the final action my left arm would successfully perform for a very long time. The inevitable impact was terrible.

That's how I saw it all happen in my mind while I watched the screw come out. In awful cinematic slow motion, I tried to yell a warning, but it was too late. The screw was out, and it all happened exactly as I saw it. The slip of the grate. The slip of Mark's ladder. The undercut of my ladder. My upending. My descent. My lame attempt to avoid being impaled by throwing the grate. The terrible impact.

The immediate noise of the crash was loud, sudden, and sickening as it continued to echo through the Hall for a few seconds. Two ladders, a screw gun, a metal grate and two grown men all hit the Church Hall floor at roughly the same moment, a cacophony of broken things.

Instant shock. Eyes closed. No words could come out, just guttural noise. The only thought was disbelief. Did that just happen? It did. What does this mean? This wasn't how you imagined your day. What next? What do you do next?

"I'M HURT!! OH, GOD! I'M HURT!"

It wasn't me saying it, but I knew I was hurt too.

Open your eyes.

"BEEJ. I'M HURT. I'M HURT BAD."

My face was pressed against the cold tile. I was looking at the ladders and tools and the grate that had scattered around me. Mark was lying next to me. My left arm was pinned below me. Get up. You must get up. You have to get help.

"Beej. Are you okay?"

"Uhhhh…yeah…I'm…I'm gonna…I gotta…I'm gonna…get help…"

Somehow, I pushed myself up with my right arm realizing my left arm didn't work. It was stuck bent at an extreme left angle. There wasn't any immediate pain, that would come later. The only thing I knew was I had to get help fast.

"Mark, I'm getting help."

I limped out of the Hall holding my left arm against my body. I couldn't move it. What did that mean? I couldn't move it at all. It was stuck. It didn't matter. I had to get help. I ran to the car and opened the door with the only good arm I had. I found myself driving to my parents' house. I approached the door exactly the moment Jubby came out. He immediately knew something was wrong. Twin power.

"What's wrong?" He could see it in my face. Not to mention I was clutching my left arm with my only working arm.

"Mark's hurt. Up in the Hall. Call for an ambulance now."

Jubby disappeared and my mother suddenly appeared.

"Brendy, what happened?"

"We fell off the ladders. Mark's hurt."

We both got in my car, this time she drove. In minutes we returned to the scene of the crime. Going back in was sickening. Mark looked like he had been spilled out all over the floor. He was unable to move. Broken ladders and debris surrounded him. Two metal grates that had recently been removed were on either side of him.

The emergency alarm came from the Town Hall. How weird. It was for us.

"Mark, help is on the way. Just stay calm," my mother was comforting him.

My job was done. I got help. What should I do next?

That was when the room started getting very bright. I knew what this was, I was fainting. I'd fainted before. It was always the same. You get dizzy. Your hearing fades away. The room gets bright and then boom, you're out. I can't faint, not now. I had to control myself and stay conscious. Instinct took over and I put my back against the wall and slid to the ground. I bent my knees toward my head. My left arm still wasn't working, it was stuck to my chest. I had to lean forward to get some blood to my head. I couldn't let myself faint. My body started shaking.

"Are you okay? Are you okay?" Somebody's face was in front of me now.

It was a paramedic.

"What's your name?" he asked.

"Brendan."

"Are you okay?"

"Yeah. I'm fine. Help Mark." I knew I was hurt but I also knew Mark was hurt way worse than me.

I sat with my back against the wall as I watched the paramedics strap Mark onto a backboard. I knew, from years of lifeguarding, they were concerned about a neck or spinal injury and were taking every precaution. Occasionally, a paramedic would come over to check on me. I tried to answer their questions, but I felt like I was going to puke.

"Did you hit your head?" somebody asked.

"I just can't move my arm," I kept saying.

They asked other questions. I tried to answer but I couldn't. I was in shock. Before long, Mark was strapped onto the backboard and being carted like so many groceries into the back of an ambulance. I climbed on board as well and sat on a bench right next to him. A paramedic sat with us checking vitals and asking us questions as the ambulance jostled toward the hospital.

"Beej, I'm sorry," Mark said with an extremely pained voice.

He wasn't just in pain. He was scared. Hell, I was scared too. He didn't look good. Was he paralyzed? Was he ever going to walk again? Why won't my arm bend? The ambulance sped down the road as we both tried to keep our cool. At one point Mark tried to steady himself by holding onto something with his hand. Unfortunately, the only item he'd be able to grab while strapped to a backboard was my conveniently located crotch. Having someone accidentally squeeze your balls while you're holding onto a broken arm must be the definition of "insult to injury."

"Sorry."

Eventually we got to the hospital and found ourselves being interviewed.

"How much pain are you in from a scale of one to ten, ten being the worst pain you've ever felt and one being no pain at all?"

"Oh, I guess a seven," Mark said.

"Crap," I thought. I was going to say that.

"How much pain are you in from a scale of one to ten?" the nurse was asking me now.

"Five?"

I didn't know. I had yet to feel any pain. The shock and adrenaline running through me was preventing it. Like I said, the pain would come later. Man, would it come.

Then Mark disappeared. He was in critical condition and would need to be helicoptered to another hospital. His injuries were extensive and life-threatening. Mark would go to a big city hospital to have his hip and pelvis repaired through surgery. He would be laid up for the better part of a year, but he'd be okay. In fact, later we discovered that the accident ironically saved his life. It turned out that Mark had a blood clot traveling through his body that would have probably caused an aneurysm and killed him. The surgeons found it and were able to put a screen in his body that saved Mark's life. Another silver lining!

I, on the other hand, would have a different journey. I was stuck in a bed surrounded by curtains in the emergency room. Nurses were coming in and out to take vitals, ask questions, take more vitals, and ask more questions. News of the accident had traveled fast and people I knew started appearing. Jubby came in. Then Aran was there. Then my parents came. A couple friends who heard what happened got to the room but were promptly escorted out.

The hospital needed to get X-rays. What a joke. The X-ray techs were asking me to do the impossible and move my arm. It wasn't happening. Having not got a single good picture, they sent me back to the emergency room. Within minutes a doctor showed up with a needle and plunged it into my arm. Then, like magic, my arm could move a little. Maybe I was fixed. Shortly thereafter, I was back in the X-ray room and pictures were taken successfully this time. Following this I was wheeled back to the emergency room feeling great about life. Not only did the shot help my arm with the X-rays, but it also took away any stress I was feeling. I was calmer than I'd ever been. That shot was incredible. More please.

The emergency room phase was over and I was wheeled to another room. It was a room with lighted screens on the wall. I just sat there doped out and waiting. I have no idea how long I waited. Time didn't seem to exist anymore. This was turning out to be the weirdest day of my life and that was saying something. I was curious where it was headed but I kind of didn't care. Like I said, that shot was incredible. My mind was in a cloud when a white-jacketed balding man with salt and pepper beard entered the room and introduced himself as Dr. Patrick Shultz. He told me he was the head orthopedic surgeon. Cool, I thought. Then the man started putting X-rays of my left elbow against the lighted screens on the wall.

"I'm very concerned," Dr. Shultz said.

This guy was not joking around. Even through the doped-out haze of the shot, I could tell that my new doctor was being very straight with me and I needed to pay attention.

"You've shattered your radial head. It's a very bad break. It'll require surgery but even after surgery...I'm not sure if your arm will ever work properly again."

Silence.

"Okay," I said.

It sounded like very bad news, and it was too heavy to process all at once. I sat there with a dazed expression trying to make sense of things. Eventually the severity of what he just told me got through to my hazy thoughts. I became worried. This was bad. This wasn't just a broken arm. My arm had been shattered. Furthermore, I had a responsibility. I was supposed to be the Best Man in Aran's wedding in a few days. That was a big deal and I didn't want to let him down.

"Can I get the surgery now?" I asked.

"I was thinking that we'd do it in a few days, actually."

"But I'm supposed to be the Best Man in my brother's wedding in a few days."

"Well…uhh. I think there's a possibility we could do it tonight. Let me check on my team's schedule."

He disappeared and within fifteen minutes returned to tell me that the surgery would in fact be performed within a few hours. Cool. I'd lived my entire life without a broken bone or major surgery. Now I was killing two birds with one stone.

The surgery was meant to pin and screw what was left of my elbow bone back together. It had truly been destroyed…blown to bits. Within the next couple hours, I'd be in and out of consciousness awaiting surgery. Eventually Dr. Shultz was suddenly above me asking me to count down from ten to one.

"Ten, nine, eight…" Darkness.

I woke up in an elevator. A nurse was above me as I lay in a bed. My left arm was wrapped up in the biggest cast I'd ever seen and chained to something that looked like a coat rack. It was pointing straight toward the ceiling. My entire arm, hand and all, were surrounded by cast. I was groggy and confused.

"Is that my arm?"

My voice sounded funny. It hurt to talk. It was hard to open my eyes.

"It is. Your surgery is over. We're wheeling you to your room to recover."

I was wheeled into the far end of a room. A window showed that it was nighttime. From what I could tell, I was on the third or fourth floor of the building. I could see city lights in the distance. To my left a pink curtain was shut. It was separating me from my new roommate.

"Use this if you have to urinate."

The nurse placed an oblong plastic bottle next to me.

"Okay."

"Press this button if you need us."

She put a small remote with a button on it in my only good hand.

"Okay."

Then she disappeared and I was alone with my newly casted arm chained straight above me and a bottle to pee in at my side. Furthermore, I was seriously doped out. The only thing I could do was pass out and hope for the best when I woke up. I might have fallen asleep for a few minutes when my neighbor, the unseen gentleman on the other side of the curtain, decided to wake me up in the worst possible way.

"Nurse! Nurse! I need help!" I would never see the poor bastard, but from the sound of his voice he was an older guy. From the aroma of the dump he had just taken in his pants, he was obviously there for some serious bowel issues.

"I shit in my pants. I need help."

The smell was terrible and the pink curtain that separated us did nothing to prevent the old man's diarrhea-filled pants from plastering the entire room with its sickening scent. I was trapped, literally chained to a pole, and stuck laying in a bed with no possibility of escape. I'd never smelled anything like it. I began gagging. Shattering your elbow is bad; being poisoned from the toxic scent of an old man's fresh feces is a fate worse than death.

"What's wrong?" It was the nurse.

"I shit my pants," the old man said.

"Let's take a look."

No. Don't look. Wheel the old man's ass out of the room.

"Oh, Jesus. I guess you did."

The nurse spent the next hour cleaning out the man's ass while I tried to keep my sanity four feet away from it all. Eventually I would pass out. When I woke up in the morning, the first thing I saw was my arm hanging from a chain directly above me. None of this was a dream. My roommate was gone and never to be seen by me. Nurses came in to explain the ins and outs of pain medication. They warned me to stay ahead of the pain. At the moment it wasn't too bad. I felt raw and fragile, but the general feeling was just a dull ache that was all over my body. Dr. Shultz came in to explain what he did during surgery. He told me I'd be in the cast for around twenty weeks and I'd be seeing a lot of him over the next few months. He said only time would tell if I'd be able to use my arm properly again. My mother showed up to take me home to heal. After all, I was the Best Man in my brother's wedding in a few days and I had duties to perform. Let me on the road to recovery.

When I got home, that was when the pain began. It was unbelievable how quickly it crept up on me. The medication took the edge off, but it didn't come close to killing it. I took as much as I dared, and everything felt very far away. However, the pain wasn't far away; it was stuck to me. The ache in my elbow was deep and inescapable. I couldn't think of anything other than the agony I was in. It was consuming every part of me. I yelled and screamed for it to go away, but it wasn't going anywhere, not for a long time. I came very close to losing my mind in those first few days after the surgery. The medication was constant and turned me into a zombie. I tried everything I could to focus my thoughts away from my suffering. The worst part was not knowing how much longer it would last. Was it going to be a week, a month, the rest of my life?

Eventually, it was the day of Aran's wedding. I was a bit of an after-thought. Jubby would be my Co-Best Man as well as my handler during the day. The agony was maddening, but I couldn't ruin my brother and his soon-to-be new wife's big day. My tuxedo shirt needed to be cut down the arm as my cast was too big to slip into it. The jacket was draped over my shoulder and my cast arm was put in a sling. I took as much medication as I was allowed to help get me through the entire event. It was going to be a long day. There would be the hour-long ceremony in the church I grew up in, then there would be the long reception in the Hall that had been the site of my accident. It was going to be a marathon and I wasn't sure I was going to make it.

The wedding was the first time I'd been out of the house since getting home from the hospital. It was a sweltering August day. Everything was far away and my mind was foggy, but I knew there would be many people attending the wedding eager to check up on me. It would be a massive crowd and I would have to talk with people all day long. This might be too much to handle. Anticipating this, I decided to take a few more pills. A thought about overdosing entered my brain, but I considered the pain I was in and swallowed the medicine. Soon, it was as if everyone was down a tunnel from me. Everything was in slow motion and hard to do. Getting from one place to another felt like a monumental task. Uh-oh. Had I taken too many drugs?

Jubby never left my side. He ushered me to the front pew as the ceremony commenced. The pain set in and steadily grew throughout the service. I rocked back and forth with my eyes closed. Please God help me. I found myself praying more intently than I ever had. I opened my eyes to look up at the life-sized crucified Jesus. He was right in front of me. I'd never had any more sympathy for his agony than I did at that moment. My pain was excruciating. It hadn't gone anywhere in days. There was no escape and I needed help. This was desperation. Jesus was on the cross right above me. Maybe he could help me out? I wasn't sure if I could survive a life of constant pain and panic set in. The ceremony was taking place and I felt broken. The pain was too much; I wasn't going to make it. One thought kept circling around in my head. Help me, help me, help me.

Then it happened.

As my older brother was saying "I do" to his new bride and my twin sat next to me, I saw the strangest sight I would ever see. As I was looking up at the full-sized statue of Jesus on the cross, something incredible happened. Jesus moved. Check that. The statue of Jesus moved. He more than moved. Jesus lifted his head from the position it had always been in, opened his eyes and looked down on me. He wasn't in pain anymore. Now his expression was peaceful.

I sat there transfixed by his stare. With compassion in his eyes, he said two words.

"It's okay."

His eyes closed and his head slowly rested back to the position the sculptor had originally intended for it to be in.

In amazement I turned to Jubby.

"Jesus just talked to me."

My twin put his arm around me. He knew how many drugs I had taken.

Did Jesus really talk to me? Was it the drugs talking? Who knows. Indians used to take a lot of peyote and try to find wisdom or advice from the spirit world. Was this any different? Jesus told me "It's okay." There was no pain in his eyes as he said it.

"It's okay."

Who was I to argue? The pain remained but the message was received. Just repeat it like a mantra. "It's okay." Believe it. Say it again and again and again. "It's okay." Keep saying it until the pain goes away. Say it until you know it in your soul. "It's okay."

And that's what I began doing. "It's okay" became my philosophy. It got me through the rest of the ceremony. It got me through the wedding reception. It even got me through my Best Man speech I forgot to prepare. The DJ handed me a microphone and commanded me to give my speech. I looked out into a sea of silent expectant faces. I decided to say the only thing I knew for sure.

"Umm, I'm on drugs. But it's okay."

Silence from over two-hundred guests for five painful seconds. Then a couple of people clapped. Then a few more. Then slow applause developed into a standing ovation. I was confused. Why are they clapping? Jubby just sat me down and finished the Best Man speech for both of us.

I got through it all. I kept thinking and saying, "It's okay." I said it for the next few weeks. I said it when I was still in agony with a giant cast imprisoning my arm for the next few months. I said it when planes were falling out of the sky on September 11th. I said it when the world seemed to be turned upside down and nobody knew how to make sense of anything. I said it over the next few months as the pain eventually receded, but my arm looked deformed and wretched. "It's okay" was getting me from day to day and moment to moment. It got me to a day, a few months after the accident, when the cast would finally come off. When it did, I was deformed and slightly crippled. My arm didn't really work very well anymore. It wasn't the same size as my other arm. My wrist couldn't turn very much, and the elbow wouldn't bend. This was my new normal, but it was okay, it had to be. There was no other way to think at this point. "It's okay" was the only way to look at things from here on out. It was my mantra.

After a few years of getting used to living with a useless arm, I began having extreme pain again. I decided to see an elbow specialist. Following a series of X-rays, he found that scar tissue had built up and broken the pin and screw from the original surgery in half. The specialist organized a new plan for me. A second surgery would have to happen. In this procedure my destroyed radial head was cut off, a hole was drilled into what remained of the bone and a prosthetic elbow, resembling a doorknob, was placed in the spot where the original bone had been. After I recovered from the second surgery, my arm, that had not worked properly in four years, began working again. I could bend my elbow all the way. I could twist my wrist the way it was meant to. The simple task of turning a doorknob could be done now when previously it had been an impossibility for years. Muscle tone came back, and I began looking like a normal human being again. It was okay, everything was.

When you're growing up you think you know what it means to be an adult. You think adulthood occurs when you reach a certain age, but, when you look back at your childhood you realize that's not true. Adulthood doesn't come from age; it comes from experience. I became an adult at twenty-five years old when my elbow was shattered into smithereens. The accident gave me the gift of perspective. I wouldn't trade my experience for anything. Before my accident I had been naïve, after it I felt different. I had a new outlook, an unshakable point of view.

Life is such a mixed bag. It is temporary and full of pain and anguish, but it's also wonderful and full of joy. Life can kick you in the teeth when you least expect it and offers a never-ending series of curveballs. There's no script and the rules are often meant to be broken.

Most of the cliches happen to be true and many of them can be used to get you through a bad day. However, I'm not sure if any cliché has ever provided an answer for the biggest question of all: What's it all about? Maybe that old saying about the journey being more important than the destination comes closest to the right answer. Our experiences make up our journey and they end up shaping us for better or worse along the way. Every experience is a gift and the best experiences end up as memories. The memories become stories. The connective tissue that exists between all the stories is a simple idea: No matter where our journey takes us, it's okay.

Epilogue: It's More Than Okay...

I fell head-over-heals in love when I was twenty-five years old. Get ready for another cliché: It was love at first sight, without a doubt. I knew I was in love with Molly the second I saw her. I'd never experienced anything like it. Our love story was a whirlwind of miracles and blessings and we knew, right away, that we needed to spend the rest of our lives together. Time moves fast with true love. You get tunnel vision, and everything becomes very clear about what matters and what doesn't matter.

Love at first sight happened again a year later when our daughter Jenna was born. Then it happened again when my daughter Mara came into the world a couple of years after that. I was in my early thirties, and I'd finally realized true happiness and my reason for being. I was put on the planet to be the best husband and father I could be. I owed it to them. Hell, I owed it to myself. And I owed it to the higher power that had given me a world of happiness and love. I had three beautiful miracles in my life. How did I deserve such blessings?

I was forty-two years old when I got the most terrifying phone call of my life.

"HONEY COME HOME NOW! OH MY GOD...THE HOUSE IS ON FIRE!" Molly was in a state of panic. I could hear chaos in the background.

"What?" I was dumbfounded. I had left my precious family two hours earlier to go to a meeting that night.

"THE HOUSE IS ON FIRE! I'M OKAY! THE GIRLS ARE OKAY! FIRE TRUCKS ARE HERE. THERE'S BLACK SMOKE POURING OUT OF THE HOUSE. JUST GET HOME."

"You're, okay?"

"Yes."

"Are the girls okay?"

"Yes. Come home now. Oh, my God. What are we going to do?" She was hysterical.

The people sitting around the table at my meeting could hear what had been coming through the other end of my phone. They were staring at me with shock in their faces. What was going on? This couldn't be happening. But it was. My beautiful world was threatened. My wife and my two girls had been in unbelievable danger, and I wasn't there to protect them.

I was dumbfounded and frozen in shock.

The man next to me grabbed my arm, "Go now. Get out of here."

Yes, go! Go now! Get home! Save your family!

I ran to the car in a dead sprint and in seconds I was roaring down the road. I was an hour away from home. The car couldn't go fast enough. My world had gone sideways, and I was completely helpless. One thought raced through my mind, "Just get home."

My cell phone was buzzing, it was Jubby.

"Where are you?"

"I'm an hour away from home. I'm driving. I just gotta get home."

My voice sounded funny. It sounded shaky and scared. I was terrified. Was Molly okay? Were my girls okay? I kept hearing the panic in Molly's voice and seeing my two little girls in their pajamas running out of a burning house. The distance between me and them at that moment was my greatest enemy.

"Just slow down. I know you're doing your best to get home, but you can't get in an accident right now."

Jubby was using his calm, professional cop voice.

"I gotta get home." That was the only thought I had.

"I know. But I just talked to Molly. She's okay. The girls are okay. Nobody's hurt. Responders are there. Just keep the car on the road. I'm leaving now and I'll meet you as soon as I can."

"Okay."

We hung up. The road became like a tunnel. I've never driven like that before. Time didn't exist. Nothing but the thought of getting to my family existed.

When I was a mile away from my house, I could see the glow of lights from dozens of ambulances and fire trucks. There was a sickening feeling in my stomach. My mind was singularly focused. Just find my girls. The sun had set below the horizon, but I could see black smoke funneling from my house. This had to be a nightmare, it couldn't be real life. I weaved my car around firefighters and rescue vehicles until I found a spot in my front lawn. It was like a scene in a movie, but this wasn't a movie. This was my life.

Somebody called out to me, "What are you doing?" It was a firefighter.

"That's my house," I yelled as I jumped out of the car.

"Where's my wife? Where are my girls?"

It was dark out but there was a strange carnival glow throughout the yard. My entire house was surrounded by hundreds of flashing lights and more fire-fighters than I'd ever seen.

"She's up by the fence," somebody pointed.

I saw her. She had our beagle Charley on a leash and a woman from the fire department was comforting her. I ran through the crowd of firefighters to get to her.

I finally reached her.

"Honey..." We just held each other. There were no words. She was beyond tears.

She was able to tell me that the girls had been picked up by a friend. They were safe. Then we watched helplessly as the fire crew went in and out of our ruined house. Black smoke was coming out of every corner. Molly and I couldn't even talk. It was too much to process. Too many questions. Our life had just been turned upside down. That was the only thing we knew.

The fire was out but our house was wrecked. The fire inspector told us that they found the cause of the blaze. A space heater in my daughter's bedroom had decided to blow up. She had been in the shower when it happened. It became immediately apparent how lucky everyone was to be able to get out of the house alive and unhurt. Later, we would spend a lot of time playing the terrible "what if" game, but for now we were in a state of pure shock. In normal life you can handle a lot of problems all at once. This was something else. You didn't even know where to start. What do we do now? Where do we live? Where do we get clothes? The questions just hovered over us. You really couldn't think about it. It was too much. Too overwhelming.

Suddenly, my entire family was there in the dark of the night. My mother and father, Aran, Jubby. We were never very much of a hugging family, but they were all hugging me that night. Our closest friends all showed up and were there for us in the darkness of the night. My phone kept going off. My bosses called to let me know that work was taken care of and not to worry about it. I eventually had to shut my phone off. I didn't have the energy.

The firefighters wrapped up their job inside the house. They gave us some advice and vanished into the night. Molly, Charley, and I were left outside the smoking burned-out shell of a house with our family and close friends.

"You're all alright. Nobody is hurt."

It was the constant refrain that came from everyone. Eventually we knew there was nothing more that could be done at that time. The night was dark. Our house was destroyed and most of our material things had been lost to fire or smoke damage. There was only one thing we knew for sure; we had to see our girls. It was the most important thing in the world at that moment. We needed to hug them with as much love as we could.

Molly and I drove away from the wreck that was our home and, in the middle of the night, we picked Jenna and Mara up from our friend's house. They had never seemed so small and fragile, but they wore brave faces. Our girls didn't know, yet, that they'd lost every possession they owned. Every toy, every stuffy, every piece of clothing, every keepsake, everything they held precious to their little hearts…all gone forever. They cried when we told them, but they also knew that we were all safe and that was what mattered. We were scared and shaken, but we were alive. None of us knew what the future was going to hold, we were running on faith.

All of us piled into the car; Molly was beside me. We were headed to her parents' house and an uncertain future. We were homeless and only had the clothes on our backs. I looked over at the woman I loved, and she looked at me. We both looked at the backseat where our beautiful little daughters were sitting on either side of Charley. Everything that mattered was in this car. That was all we needed. Molly and I both knew one thing, and we knew it with absolute certainty, everything was going to be okay.

But, for some reason, something also felt different. There was a sense of calm. We were safe. We were alive. We were healthy and we were together. In the darkness of the night, we drove toward our uncertain future thinking the same thing.

Life was more than okay, *it was great.*

9 798385 128242